MISSION THEOLOGY
TODAY

JOHN POWER, S.M.A.

ORBIS BOOKS
MARYKNOLL, NEW YORK

Printed in the United States of America

CONTENTS

INTRODUCTION   vi

PART I—WHY MISSIONS?

CHAPTER 1. THE ROOTS OF DISCONTENT   3

        2. A NEW VISION OF THE CHURCH   14

        3. A CHURCH ESSENTIALLY MISSIONARY   33

        4. MISSIONS—AN OLD TESTAMENT IDEAL   59

        5. THE NEW TESTAMENT—A MISSIONARY
            MANDATE   78

PART II—DIDACHE, DEVELOPMENT AND THE FUTURE

        6. SALVATION AND NON-CHRISTIAN RELIGIONS   99

        7. EVANGELISATION AND RELIGIOUS FREEDOM   118

        8. DEVELOPMENT AS A MISSIONARY TASK   137

        9. THE PRIMACY OF PROCLAMATION   159

       10. SIGNPOSTS TO THE FUTURE   173

       11. THE MISSIONARY MENTALITY   194

        Appendices—(a) Official Text of Symposium
                       Conclusions   211

                   (b) List of Theologians   217

INTRODUCTION

It was a cold March evening in the stylish Rome suburb of EUR, with its striking architectural memories of Mussolini's days and the 1960 Olympic Games. To the Seraphicum, the quiet studentate of the Conventuals, a steady stream of cars carried members of most of the international Generalates of Sisters, Fathers and Brothers in Rome. The several hundreds in the Aula Magna that evening formed a group which could fairly claim to be representative of the Church's present missionary effort. They had assembled for the opening of a four-day symposium on the theme: Mission Theology for our Times.

They heard Fr Monde, Superior General of the Society of African Missions and President of SEDOS, in his address of welcome, explain frankly and clearly why the symposium had been arranged:

> It must be said, without equivocation, that the missionary institutes are preoccupied, worried and uncertain about the future of missions. This is not to indulge in pessimism. In a changing world which daily poses new problems, it is perfectly normal that the missionary world also should ask questions about its own function in this rapid and often radical evolution.

Next, Cardinal Agagianian, the Cardinal Prefect of the Congregation for the Evangelisation of Peoples, expressed the hope that serious studies such as the SEDOS symposium would help to dissipate the crisis of confidence 'at present affecting the Church's missionary calling and task', so that we could soon witness 'a renewal of missionary enthusiasm based on firm convictions and directed towards the great perspectives thrown open by the command of the Lord Jesus: "Euntes in mundum universum, praedicate evangelium omni creaturae".' And immediately the symposium got under way, with the first conference, 'The Newness of the Gospel', given by Fr Stanislaus Lyonnet, S.J., Vice-Rector of Rome's Biblical Institute.

That March evening was the culmination and fruit of two years of hoping and planning by the SEDOS institutes. SEDOS is a co-operative venture on the part of a number of missionary institutes, through which they aim at closer and more efficient collaboration in practical apostolic activity. Its ultimate purpose is to ensure that different institutes in the same mission territory will be able to work together directly on common projects and problems, and thus make more effective use of their combined resources of manpower and means. In most mission countries several institutes work side by side. But much of the time they work quite independently, with little or no exchange of information between them. To improve this situation is precisely the aim of SEDOS.

SEDOS was founded in June 1964, and now numbers over thirty missionary institutes, male and female. The name comes from the Italian title: Servizio di Documentazione e Studi (Documentation and Study Service), and reflects the primary concern of the member institutes—to plan and work together on the basis of a scientific study of contemporary mission facts and trends. At the frequent SEDOS meetings every aspect of missionary activity is freely aired and examined. This is a more comprehensive and frank exchange of missionary experiences, problems, experiments, obstacles and successes than could have been even imagined in the pre-Vatican II era. As a result of this continual exchange of information and experiences, the contacts between the member institutes have grown more practical, more frequent and more fruitful.

The idea of a theological meeting to discuss missions was first put forward at a SEDOS reunion in February 1967. In spite of much preliminary hesitation, it gathered momentum and support under the active stewardship of the then President of SEDOS, Fr Schutte, S.V.D. As the SEDOS members discussed the project they became increasingly convinced that mission theology had remained an under-developed area, even after the Vatican Council. Professional theologians had said or written almost nothing about the missionary aspects of the

Church's renewed self-consciousness. This is a lacuna that so far has not been filled either by missionaries themselves or by missiologists. The fundamental questions are strictly theological ones—the essentially missionary nature of the Church, the obligation of preaching the gospel to all men. Thus SEDOS turned to the theologians for help.

Eventually, the shape of the meeting was determined. It would not be a series of lectures to a public audience, like the missiological StudyWeeks held at Louvain, Burgos and Milan. Rather, SEDOS aimed at a closed discussion of a few well-defined topics by a selected group of internationally-known theologians. It would not be a discussion between professional missiologists on questions of method, but between theologians of differing interests and specialities, each of whom would be asked to bring his special training and talents to bear on basic missionary questions. And SEDOS insisted that they should be drawn from the whole Catholic world, not merely Europe.

However, because good theologians are rare they are normally overworked. Several of the eminent scholars invited were unfortunately unable to participate, including Fathers Küng, Congar, Dulles, Mackenzie, Rahner, Schillebeeckx and Thils. When a team of theologians was finally assembled, each was sent a list of possible topics—all of them aspects of the basic question: Why missions?—and asked for comments and suggestions. As a result of these, the list was narrowed down to two central themes, both uppermost in the minds of missionaries at present: the precise value of non-Christian religions as roads to salvation; the place of development work in missionary activity.

On these two topics a series of conferences was prepared by the participating theologians, and a lengthy discussion period was allowed after each one. A list of the theologians is given in an appendix. One of them was Fr Jean Daniélou, whose writing on mission themes over the past twenty years is known everywhere, and the happiest moment of the symposium was the announcement of his elevation to the College of Cardinals.

This book is not the text of the symposium lectures; its aim is more modest and its range more limited. But it was originally inspired by the symposium, it has grown directly out of it, and it uses most of the material presented there. It is an attempt to put into simple words the conclusions reached by the theologians, some of the arguments on which the conclusions were based, and some of the suggestions put forward in papers and discussions.

There is no claim to comprehensive treatment of the vital issues involved; that would be a formidable task requiring a far different book and a far better author. This is rather the unpretentious meditation of a missionary on the subject of missions and of why we must continue to devote every energy to our missionary task. It is limited to the great theological themes on which our missionary work is based—the ultimate 'why' of missions and our individual missionary dedication. Because the symposium confined itself to theological questions, this book has nothing to say about the applied practical problems of apostolic methods or priorities.

The first section is really an attempt to provide the necessary background to the theologians' treatment of their themes. Since it is comparatively easy to be side-tracked from the central issue by technicalities and theological nuances, the opening chapters are devoted to the simple, foundational and infinitely comforting biblical themes of the People of God, the universality of the Father's love for his children, and the vibrant missionary dynamism of the New Testament. In the following section we attempt, in spite of the risks involved, to reproduce the argumentation of the theologians, but in shorter and less technical form.

This is not a book for experts or professors; it is directed exclusively to busy missionaries who have neither the time nor the opportunity to keep abreast of the contemporary torrent of writing on such topics as the Church and the non-Christian religions. It is directed especially to the thousands of untrumpeted heroes, men and women, of the missionary world of today, who work hard and unobtrusively in little bush parishes and schools, but who suffer because of the multiplicity of vague question-marks that float in the theological air. They suffer quietly, silently. They are members neither of an articulate protesting minority nor of a smugly eloquent majority. But they are painfully aware that the clear, magisterial theological tones of other and earlier days have given way to clamorous controversy, difficult to understand but impossible to disregard.

In the current demand for specialists and generalists, they feel elbowed aside, but are too humble to protest. In the battle of words about subjects like catechetical methods they feel inadequate, but bow to supposedly superior intellects. In the prolonged academic discussions about the role of development, they, non-specialists and non-technicians, wonder if they have not become out-dated, but follow their better instincts and continue to preach the gospel to their little flocks. In the search for publicity and the rush to the microphone, they are in danger of becoming the neglected ones, a 'fourth world' of unwanted and old-fashioned idealists. Bewildered but tenacious, they cling to Matthew's final verses and Paul's insistent theme, but do so in spite of rather than because of the theological experts, from whom they receive little attention and no encouragement. For them, the real preachers of the gospel in our complicated day, this little book has been written—in sympathy and tribute.

It would be impossible to indicate all who have helped. I have leaned heavily on the French missionary publication *Spiritus*, and have consistently regretted that there is nothing comparable in the English language. Scriptural quotations are taken from the Jerusalem Bible; Vatican II quotations are taken from *The Documents of Vatican II*, edited by Fr Abbott, S.J. Fr Abbott is now Director of the Vatican Office for Common Bible Work in the Secretariat for Promoting Christian Unity, and I am deeply grateful to him for sharing so readily with me his incomparable knowledge and experience in matters ecumenical. My special gratitude goes to Fr Douau and Fr Gantly of the S.M.A. Central Secretariat, confrères who responded to my many calls for help with articles, advice and admirable patience.

PART I

Why Missions ?

1 The Roots of Discontent

It is a relatively new experience for missionaries to be asked to justify the value of their work. They had grown accustomed to being regarded as the highly respected Foreign Legion of the Church militant, returning home occasionally from the far-flung outposts to rest a little and perhaps bask a little in the admiration of devout stay-at-home Catholics. It was accepted as an axiom that missionary work was the highest form of Christian charity, and Pius XI's phrase came readily to the lips of most mission promoters: 'Of all the works of the Catholic Church the greatest and holiest is that of the Missions. This work surpasses other forms of charity as much as the soul surpasses the body.'

But these are new days. We are being asked to prove the usefulness of what we are doing. Where we used to talk about our missionary duties we now have to defend our missionary rights. It is being suggested, and none too subtly, that missionary activity has out-lived its purpose and its era, and that we are rapidly becoming redundant. This change in attitude has caused anxiety all over the Christian world. In presenting the document on the missions at the Council, the late Cardinal Bea said: 'Doubts have arisen on all sides, for different reasons, regarding the opportuneness and the need of missionary activity properly speaking. The Schema must tackle this danger and provide a remedy.' About the same time, Dr Visser 't Hooft lamented at a meeting of the World Council of Churches that 'nearly all the signs in the realm of politics and ideas point to the direction of increasing rather than decreasing unwillingness to recognise the raison d'être of missions'. One alarmed theologian summed it up succinctly: 'Formerly the mission had problems; today it has itself become a problem.'

Obviously, for missionaries themselves this generates a radical and fundamental anguish. It is bad enough to have a difficult job to do, but much worse when one is left wondering if the difficult job is worth doing. This new uncertainty about the purpose and value of missionary activity stems from a variety of causes. Historical facts and theological thinking have converged to bring the situation to crisis-point in the present decade.

Historical Facts

The first of these is that the colonial era has ended. The flags of the European empire-builders have been hauled down, and the sun now sets on a multiplicity of new countries stepping into nationhood and international recognition. Many of these are countries where, up to recently, the missionary worked side by side with his fellow-European civil servants and government officials, and where he could, if necessary, find a certain shelter under the wing of a tolerant if not enthusiastic empire. It must be said, in justice, that most missionaries at all times were uninterested in politics, and were careful to maintain a clear distinction between their activity and that of the colonial administration and commercial concerns. Still, it is not insignificant that the late Tom Mboya could write in 1963 that the social life of the missionaries 'has often reflected the behaviour of the European settlers and colonial administrators, and disenchantment has come when nationalists see in the missionary world itself' the same system and attitude which prevail among the settlers'.

The missionary Church now finds herself working, for the most part, in small, newly independent countries. Understandably, all young countries are sensitive, intensely aware of their new-found national character and conscious, perhaps for the first time, of their local culture. They are extremely sensitive to criticism, no matter how constructive and friendly, especially if it comes from an 'outsider'. The people we meet in these countries finally feel themselves free to mould their own political destinies, and they are no longer willing to accept patronising advice or peremptory commands. Perhaps nothing will recall us missionaries so sharply to our original function of service as the experience of living and working in this new atmosphere, but the process will often be accompanied by considerable frustration and even humiliation.

By an accident of history, the end of the colonial era coincides with the end, at least to a certain extent, of an era in missionary activity. The great missionary endeavour of founding the Church where it did not previously exist is largely at an end; we can say that the Church is now present in almost every country of the world. Many missionaries must now turn to deal with a new situation: that of helping to bring the young churches to their true maturity. The missionary, in this context, is clearly the auxiliary, the curate, the helper, the humble servant of the young local church, helping to guide it forward towards full maturity and independence as an ecclesial unit. This is still genuine and deeply rewarding missionary work, but work over which the missionary no longer presides as the undisputed director; he continues to row the boat but he no longer steers it. And for the missionary this often means, simply and bluntly, that he has lost many of his privileges but has retained all his obligations.

However, at this point two remarks must be made. First, change as such is a normal condition of the created universe we inhabit. It is merely a healthy sign of life, a sign of the continuing evolution of all things, a sign that a questing humanity is ever on the move. And change is generally accompanied by crisis, to some extent or other. The great religious changes in history all generated crisis, and the crisis in turn hastened the moment of change: the arrival of Christianity, the Reformation, the 'new' post-conciliar Church. Crisis is the human price of progress; we must be willing to pay it. Besides, change and crisis are creative, taxing our skills and ingenuity, forcing us to produce new and fresh ideas and to adopt courageous experiments.

Second, the change in the ecclesiastical situation in mission countries—the appearance of the local church—is really a tribute to the effectiveness of past missionary labours. This change springs, not from a mistake or a mishap, but from our own success to date. It is, in fact, a giant stride forward towards the final goal of all missionary endeavour.

Another change in the traditional missionary image and status results from the vastly increased activity of highly organised philanthropic agencies. The 'third world' has caught the imagination, not merely of kind-hearted private citizens, but of official and international organisations. When the communications media talk about mission territories, which they do more than ever before, it is almost always from the point of view of the third world, and in terms of political and sociological conditions. Time was when the missionary was the only pillar of socio-economic development in his limited region, and, amateur though he was, he often performed signs and wonders with almost non-existent means and against stubborn obstacles. Now, international organisations and government agencies have stepped into the breach, with a technical competence and resources in finance and personnel far beyond the dreams of the most optimistic missionary. Huge welfare programmes have taken over one of the fringe activities of every zealous missionary. Later on, we shall raise the question of the missionary's involvement in development work as an integral part of his apostolic activity.

Again, it is possible to be depressed beyond measure by the so-called 'statistical' argument against missions. It goes something like this: figures and statistics prove that missionaries are fighting a losing battle. Today, two thousand years after Christ, there are more than 2,000 million non-Christians, and the number constantly increases. The population explosion is greatest precisely in the under-developed countries; thus, if we except South America, among the non-Christians. If one were to judge by the demographic data, we are in a hopeless situation. To what purpose do we continue to struggle, if all the calculations and statistics show that our work cannot, in spite of our best efforts, achieve any substantial change in a movement set on an apparently immutable course? According to an American study, in 1954 Catholics numbered 19·1 per cent of the world's population; in 1956, 18·3 per cent; and in 1958, 18·2 per cent. We must look reality in the face: the Christian missionary movement is not able to keep pace with the galloping demographic increase. Thus, a Church universal by its nature seems destined to remain forever a feeble minority. In that case, where is the urgency of our missionary task?

Finally, among the 'signs of the times' that agitate missionary institutes, none is so disquieting and discouraging as the universal decrease in vocations in the mission-sending countries. Many anguished analyses of this phenomenon are being made all over Europe and North America. The reasons for it range from sociological factors like the affluence of society to religious ones, chiefly a faith growing cold. Whatever the real reasons—and they are probably multiple—the fact is painfully clear, and for missionary institutes it means, simply and severely, that as their commitments and opportunities grow their numbers shrink. This is particularly disturbing to the missionaries in the field, who are forced to wonder if their work and its fruits have entered a gloomy cul-de-sac, and if they are left to contemplate the lingering twilight of what was a glorious day.

Theological Thinking

The development of theology, the deepening of human understanding of the content of revelation, the clarifying of man's insights into the ways and wonders of God, is necessarily a slow process. Various currents of theological thought which had been quietly gathering momentum for over twenty years finally and triumphantly found expression in the documents of Vatican II. It is true that every missionary, no matter how remote his bush station or how insignificant his parish statistics, found immense comfort and joy in the Council declarations. But, at the same time, he would candidly admit that, from some points of view, he got much from the Council that he did not quite expect, and he can be forgiven for feeling, at least occasionally, that even theology had turned traitor to the missionary cause. Let us enumerate some of the difficulties with which Vatican II and its aftermath presented him.

One of the great statements of the Council was that the whole Church is missionary by its very nature. Quickly it went on to draw a conclusion from that: 'Every disciple of Christ has the obligation to do his part in spreading the faith.' But where does this leave this vibrant human being that we call the average missionary? Certainly, it leaves him bereft of the older, more romantic picture of himself as the pioneer who manned the remote outposts of Christ's kingdom on earth. Now he is the same as every baptised Christian, another one of the Church's millions of missionaries. His monopoly has vanished overnight, and he can now sit on his lonely verandah and wonder why he suffers the pangs of exile and the stings of mosquitoes, if he could have been equally a missionary in his native diocese.

Another conclusion from the missionary nature of the Church is that the universal Church expresses and executes its missionary duty through the whole College of Bishops. 'The responsibility to proclaim the gospel throughout the world falls primarily on the body of bishops' (*Ad Gentes*, art. 29). This splendid theological insight does, however, present the missionary institutes with some problems in their home countries. Since the College of Bishops is represented in a particular country by the National Episcopal Conference, in what sense or to what degree is the activity of the missionary institutes to be channelled through these Episcopal Conferences? Will a missionary on his arrival home, for example, discover that he is unable to preach to or exhort the good people of his own parish or diocese about his work and his hopes, and instead find himself referred to a kind of anonymous Vocations Committee or Mission Council —the faceless men of a new ecclesiastical bureaucracy? Is the personal witness, the spontaneity of a missionary's live experience of the working of God's love in a pagan country, to be drained of all its content and warmth and reduced to another name and statistic in a chancery register? Surely these are not the ways of a Church daily being reminded of its inner charismatic nature and its providential diversity of ministries.

The Council declarations on non-Christian religions, on religious freedom, on ecumenism, have all caused missionaries to re-think many of their traditional positions. In discussion, many find it more and more difficult to hold that Christians have a more efficient or easier way to salvation than non-Christians. And here, without doubt, is the hinge of the contemporary mission crisis: the conflict between the accessibility of salvation outside the visible Church and the traditional vigorous policy of conversion. If membership of the Church does not at least provide a surer way to salvation, then what meaning can our missionary effort have?

So many inaccuracies and exaggerations have crept into print in the past few years on the subject of other religions as ways of salvation that it is often difficult to separate the chaff from the wheat. However, we have lived happily for a long time with the idea that salvation, in its full sense, is a Christian prerogative.

And this was always a primary motive in evangelisation.Where do we stand, now that this motive seems to have evaporated in the heat of conciliar enthusiasm? The motive of the salvation of souls by conversion to the Church, which sent St Francis Xavier and all the great missionaries out across the world, does not seem to carry much conviction any more. If every man has the possibility of finding God in his own religion, why convert him from it? It would seem more logical and more realistic to help him live his own religion better and follow its observances more faithfully. Is this the dialogue with non-Christians that we are being urgently advised to undertake?

Closely allied to this is the even more sensitive area of ecumenism. *Lumen Gentium* has this to say about our fellow-Christians of other denominations: 'They lovingly believe in God the Father Almighty and in Christ, Son of God and Saviour. They are consecrated by baptism through which they are united with Christ' (art. 15). A missionary is justified in demanding: Are all Christian religions of equal value, or are they not? If we exchange pulpits, can we not also exchange catechumens? It is unfortunate but true that in many mission territories the extension of Christianity took the form of a race between different Christian denominations, each rushing to establish its own churches and schools in more and more areas. What is the missionary to do in this new ecumenical climate — withdraw gracefully from the race?

The Council document on religious freedom, *Dignitatis Humanae,* can also pose problems. Missionaries do not make Christians by the sword, it is true, and they have no desire to exert undue pressure or influence on prospective converts. But the suggestion has been put forward, in several subtle forms, that the statement 'the human person has a right to religious freedom' (*Dig. Hum.,* art. 2) is irreconcilable with our desire to preach the gospel to all and to attract men to the faith.While it is easy to show that this is false, at first sight it does seem to

provide yet another painful dilemma for the harassed missionary who is trying hard to bring men to the knowledge of the
truth.

One further consequence of the conciliar documents should
be added: the emphasis on the apostolate of the laity. The
advent of lay missionaries is, of course, the fulfilment of a long-
felt desire, and every missionary will welcome the tremendous
assistance they can give. But it does raise the question: why be a
priest missionary if one can be equally effective as a lay missionary? From this point of view it almost certainly is a contributing
factor to the decrease in vocations. And as such it constitutes a
serious preoccupation for the priest whose parish is too big,
whose out-stations are too numerous, and who can hope to see
some of his flock only twice a year. And he may be forgiven for
wondering if this is not still another incursion of the secular city
on his hitherto sacred domain.

This is, for better or worse, the age of specialisation. We have
placed our available laurel wreaths on the heads of the tech-
nicians and crowned them 'with glory and splendour'. The
specialist is the current god, and we make daily acts of faith in
his pontifications. The Church, plunged into the heart of the
modern world as never before, can neither avoid nor ignore this
trend. Thus a constant stream of appeals issues from the Roman
Congregations and from the religious institutes for more
specialists—in catechetics, liturgy, sociology, missiology. All
this is good, useful and holy, but we must in fairness ask: are
we at the same time being just to the average hard-working
missionary who is neither specialist nor technician? Is this good
man, who does most of the hard, unrewarding drudgery,
achieves the real results and asks none of the publicity, to be left
in exterior darkness? There is a danger that, in the clamour for
experts, the truly pastoral missionary may be made to feel
merely an abandoned relic of a simpler but vanished era.

This impression may be heightened when he comes home on

holidays and discovers that the interest of people in missionary problems and progress has changed. It is not that it has necessarily become less; it has simply become different. The emphases have shifted. Again, the missionary may find himself on the defensive—trying to give reasons for his work. There was a time when missionary magazines and promotion talks relied almost exclusively on the venerable repertoire of traditional mission stories—the perils from poisonous reptiles, the adventures of putting the roof on the new church. Now they find that this simple 'snakes-and-ladders' approach can be worse than useless, capable of provoking only yawns or jeers. The questions people ask about missions have become more serious, more fundamental, more searching—and more difficult to answer. But answer them we must; our survival as a credible apostolic community demands this.

These are some of the developments that can prove disturbing to the overworked missionary, who is likely to be aware of all the criticisms but not of all the replies. In order to restore our missionary self-confidence, in order to regain that sense of urgency that first sent us out, it is necessary to take a closer look at some of these problems in the following chapters. We can promise no easy answers—but perhaps this is just as well. Clear thinking and a genuine search for truth can be hampered by the too-easy answers, the general, radical, extremist solutions. And these are almost always wrong, because extreme solutions are normally based on only one aspect of a many-sided problem. The easy answer, the oh-so-simple universal remedy, is rarely right, because life is a complex entity, human beings are infinite in their variety, and circumstances change from day to day and from country to country.

We can only hope to give some samples of the current theological understanding of the problems, the tentative solutions being proposed, and to indicate the areas where no consensus of opinion has yet been reached. But even from that it will emerge that there is no reason for pessimism among missionaries or missionary institutes, and that, by their courageous meeting of their present difficulties, missionary activity will find itself at the door of a new and brighter future.

2 A New Vision of the Church

It is difficult to justify yet another attempt to say something about the nature of the Church. So much has been written on this subject in recent years, and commentaries on *Lumen Gentium* are so numerous, that a synopsis is impossible and an addition unnecessary. Still, a theologian writing in 1967 could bemoan in all earnestness that ecclesiology is the most under-developed dogmatic area of theology today. And, of course, the clarity of understanding is not necessarily measured by the volume of writing.

In any case, the aim of this chapter is extremely modest: to suggest once again, and in the simplest possible terms, some of the Council's insights on the Church that have a direct bearing on our missionary work and motives. Therefore the reference is chiefly to two documents: *Lumen Gentium* on the Church and *Ad Gentes* on the Missions. But the references are brief and made in passing, and are intended only to serve as reminders.

Perhaps the newness of the Council's vision of the Church is best illustrated by contrasting it with the general pre-conciliar approach. For purposes of contrast, here is a rapid outline of the argumentation in a typical textbook of mission theology in the twenty years before Vatican II. Starting from the text 'As the Father sent me, so am I sending you' (*John* 20:21), the author proceeds to the Church as the seat of a visible authority, one and authentic, which will assure the diffusion of Christ's message in perfect uniformity. This will be done by planting the visible Church in every place, which is the object of missionary activity. Missionaries have the aim of promoting the Church as the possessor of truth, the source and distributor of the means of salvation. Missionary activity proceeds from the virtue of religion, to which, according to St Thomas, belongs the building up of the kingdom of God.

We recall this older missiological approach, not by any means to make fun of it, but simply to indicate how radically the theological climate has altered since that line of argument was put into print before World War II. Even more interesting—and welcome—is the change that is coming about in the concept of missions as an integral part of ecclesiology. Up to the first decades of the twentieth century, books and articles on the Church rarely mentioned missions. For example, Billot's classic textbook on the Church devotes only twelve pages out of 700 to the Church's mission. And the venerable *Dictionnaire de Théologie Catholique* contains no article on missions.

This situation improved only when the theological vision of the Church began to change and expand. It then became evident that the concept of missions proposed by the great missiologists like Charles and Schmidlin was incomplete, because it did not emerge as an integral part of a theology of the Church. Only by seeing her own nature as essentially dynamic could the Church fully understand the inner necessity of her missionary dynamism. And this is precisely what is expressed in the documents of Vatican II.

In *Lumen Gentium*, for example, the very tone of the approach and the whole tenor of the argument are so refreshingly different from those of older ecclesiological statements. The viewpoint is more humble and more human. This is the Church looking at herself; not presenting herself imperiously and proudly to humanity but undertaking, in humility and honesty, a careful examination of conscience. *Lumen Gentium* is a document hammered out after long debate and much re-writing, 'an unprecedented venture in ecclesiological self-examination and self-understanding', as one of the non-Catholic observers at the Council expressed it. Again, it speaks a language far different from that of earlier Councils. Legalistic definitions and scholastic distinctions have no place here. This is strong, colourful, vivid, intensely biblical language, in the style and spirit of Christ's parables and Paul's letters. It is realistic and honest. The Church is presented, not as an élite of exalted souls, but as a servant community composed of frail and fickle men, whose only and adequate hope is God's measureless love for them.

Its openness to the whole thirsting world is revealed even in the choice of opening words and therefore of title. The phrase is obviously borrowed from the Canticle of Simeon, one of Luke's unashamedly missionary canticles: 'the salvation which you have prepared for all the nations to see, a light to enlighten the pagans'—Luke 2:30–31. In fact, the opening phrases of the document leave us in no doubt that this is intended to be a missionary ecclesiology. 'Christ is the light of all nations. Hence this most sacred Synod, which has been gathered in the Holy Spirit, eagerly desires to shed on all men that radiance of His which brightens the countenance of the Church. This it will do by proclaiming the gospel to every creature.' The note of universality is struck at once: all nations, all men, every creature. With a statement that is thus simultaneously biblical, christological and missionary, the Constitution on the Church is off to a promising start.

These preliminary and superficial impressions are confirmed and consolingly deepened as soon as we settle down to a slow, careful reading of the texts of *Lumen Gentium* and *Ad Gentes*. For our present purpose we can limit ourselves to three themes:

>   the Church as the People of God;
>   the Church as a pilgrim Church;
>   the Church as essentially missionary.

The People of God

This is one of the foundational themes running through, and at the basis of, all the conciliar documents, and so it is not surprising that it formed the starting-point of most of the conferences of the symposium. However, it would be misleading to think that this was a new discovery of the Council. It is, on the contrary, a deeply biblical idea which, long buried under layers of more juridic titles, was increasingly re-discovered by theologians during the twenty-five years preceding Vatican II. The great Yves Congar, in a study written in 1937, was one of the first to point out the importance and value of this concept as a means towards a better understanding of the nature of the Church. Articles in the same strain began to appear in France and Germany immediately. Their common aim was to break free from the static conception of a Church founded once for all by Christ, and search the Scriptures for the slow development of God's saving plan. This involved a clear understanding of the continuity of the Church with Old Testament Israel, and a willingness to view the Church in the larger perspective of the full range of salvation history. On Fr Congar's own evidence this trend of thought was helped forward during the pre-war years by the growing liturgical movement and by the new lay enthusiasm expressed through Catholic Action. It is hardly an accident that at present the Church's new understanding of herself should coincide with a new era in liturgical thinking and with a new awareness of the apostolate of the laity.

The professional theologians became interested, and a new theological dimension was gradually added to traditional thinking about the Church. Cerfaux, for instance, published his *Theology of the Church in the Writings of St Paul* in 1942. Basing his arguments strictly and scientifically on the New Testament writings, he showed that St Paul did not present the concept of body as the fundamental one by which he would, if asked, define the Church. Paul began from the Jewish idea of Israel as the People of God, the people to whom belonged the promises, the knowledge and the worship of the one true God. It was chiefly to express the profound unity in Christ of the different local churches that Paul appealed to the analogy of body. This is, then, really an attribute of the Church, but the basic definition remains People of God.

However, as Paul VI said in opening the second session of the Vatican Council: 'The Church is a mystery. It is a reality imbued with the hidden presence of God. It lies, therefore, within the very nature of the Church to be always open to new and greater exploration.' Thus there seems neither need nor excuse for a testy controversy between the merits of the titles 'People of God' and 'Mystical Body'. These are not contradictory titles jostling one another for our approval; they are both soundly biblical, and both are necessary, and even both together are inadequate to convey the richness of the notion of Christ's Church. The relationship between them is one of simple complementarity. Both of them represent St Paul's heroic efforts to overcome the poverty of human language struggling to express the splendour of divine realities.

The People of God is the picture of herself that the present-day Church has chosen to express her nature and her function in the world. All chapter 2 of *Lumen Gentium* is worth much re-reading and leisurely reflection. This is true for everybody, but especially so for a missionary. Here it is enough to mention two aspects of this 'People of God' theme: the profoundly biblical foundations of the idea; some of the consequences for our missionary ministry.

The children of Israel became the People of God by the historic intervention of Yahweh on their behalf in the exodus from Egypt and the alliance at Sinai. God does not act through abstractions but through events in human history. It is important to remember that Israel did not become the People of God simply by becoming aware of it; this psychological awareness would be merely an illusion of grandeur if it were not founded on historical fact. Only slowly did Israel achieve real consciousness of her true relationship to Yahweh, and it took many centuries of prayerful reflection and of prophetic proclamation before she understood the dignity and the responsibility of her function as People of God. Thus, to grasp her understanding of it we must look back to the events of Sinai through the evaluation of them contained in the later Old Testament writings.

Probably the best summary is that found in chapter 26 of Leviticus. This chapter forms the conclusion to what is commonly called the 'Code of Holiness'—a set of laws apparently codified during the period of the kings but re-written in its present form after the return from the exile. Chapter 26 itself contains several echoes of Ezekiel's preaching during the exile. From that vantage-point, this is how the Israelites understood God's action at the Sea of Reeds and Mount Sinai:

> I will set up my dwelling among you, and I will not cast you off. I will live in your midst; I will be your God and you shall be my people. It is I, Yahweh your God, who have brought you out of the land of Egypt so that you should be their servants no longer. I have broken the yoke that bound you and have made you walk with head held high (*Lev*. 26:11-13).

Thus, the events at Sinai, described in Exodus 19-24, had far more wonderful results than the collection of fleeing slaves at the foot of the mountain could possibly have understood. This was not a transitory meeting with God; it was the inauguration of a permanent relationship: 'I will set up my dwelling among you.' For an Israelite this was a tremendous mystery to grapple with—the transcendent Yahweh of the heavens living among his earthbound people. But his help had been so constant and his interventions so frequent that the Israelites could only conclude that he was walking beside them through their troubled history. Also, they were constantly being reminded that their presence in the Promised Land was due entirely to God; he broke 'the yoke that bound you', he 'brought you out of the land of Egypt'. In all the events of salvation history the initiative lies with God. God called men, God made a covenant with them, God supported them. It is God who finds men, not men who find God. This is a truth we need to be reminded of today.

Because the Israelites were called by God and covenanted with God, they enjoyed a new status and accepted new responsibilities. They were no longer their own, moving towards a destination of their own choice. They were no longer merely the people of Israel; they were now the People of God. By the alliance God had committed himself to be their God, and they had promised to be his people, and to walk towards him 'with head held high'. They should walk proudly, not because they possessed a land and a king, but because they had a unique and privileged relationship with the only God, a relationship which was not shared by other men.

This privilege, naturally, involved corresponding obligations. By accepting the Sinai alliance—'we will obey' (*Exod.* 24:7)—they had assumed the responsibility of becoming a community, an 'assembly', as the Old Testament calls it, using the term later translated as 'church'. It was to be a community of hope, because their whole new way of life was based on the promises of Yahweh, who had led them out from a hostile land and guaranteed them a home. It was to be a community of experience, welded together by the hardships of war and the sweet taste of independence. But, all the time, they were experiencing God, seeing his ways, savouring the immensity of his affection for his people. They had opportunities, too, of gauging the careful justice of a good father, as Yahweh allowed them to suffer some of the effects of their own infidelity. Divisive forces

were always in danger of rending the community asunder:
twelve tribes, two kingdoms, false prophets. But God's attitude
to his people remained: 'I will not cast you off.' It is interesting
that this conviction grew stronger rather than weaker during
the exile in Babylon. Perhaps it will always be true that his
people learn more about their God in adversity than in pros-
perity.

> If Yahweh had not been on our side
> —let Israel repeat it—
> if Yahweh had not been on our side
> when they attacked us,
> they would have swallowed us alive
> and burnt us to death in their rage (*Ps.* 124:1–3).

The term 'People of God' describes a community of men
called together by God to be his own, held together by their
historical experiences of his care for them, and bound to him by
an alliance—his promises and their response. It was a small
community, numerically and geographically. It was a poor
community, in terms of both wealth and culture, by contrast
with some of its neighbouring empires. It was a community
that learned slowly, and only an infinitely patient God could
have continued to call it his people. It was a community that
suffered many internal crises as well as external defeats, but was
never obliterated. Is it not a source of encouragement to look
back to this primitive community and realise that, for all its
faults and errors, it was still chanting the praises of its God in
temple and synagogue when the Lord came?
Theologians are often diplomatically vague when they come
to discuss the precise relationship between Israel as the ancient
People of God and the Church of Christ as the new People of
God. Many simply declare that the Church is the new Israel—
and hurry on. But it is only honest to say straight away that the

expression 'the new Israel' is not found anywhere in the New Testament. However, a single text, or the lack of it, does not alone constitute an argument; we must take the whole range of New Testament thought into account. Here we encounter immediately the core of the problem. On the one hand, the new People of God is the lawful continuation of the Old Testament People of God; without hesitation St Paul applies the text of Leviticus 26:12 already quoted to his young Christian communities. '. . . that is what we are—the temple of the living God. We have God's word for it: I will make my home among them and live with them; I will be their God and they shall be my people' (2 *Cor.* 6:16).

On the other hand, the New Testament People of God is emphatically a new creation, the fruit of Christ's redemptive action. For Christ's contemporaries it certainly represented not merely a discontinuity but an abrupt change, and the Jews saw themselves for the most part excluded from the new People of God because of their refusal to accept Jesus as the Messiah. Here is the source of Paul's anguish, so dramatically expressed in Romans 9–11. 'What I want to say is this: my sorrow is so great, my mental anguish so endless, I would willingly be condemned and be cut off from Christ if it could help my brothers of Israel, my own flesh and blood' (*Rom.* 9:2–3).

The New Testament evidence, then, shows that the true relationship between the old and the new People of God is one of promise-fulfilment. While we find comfort and light in the fact that our Church is rooted in the ancient promises to Israel, we must not think in terms of the simple continuity of Old Testament prerogatives. The element we must isolate and emphasise is the newness of Christ's Church, the newness of the gospel message. The redemption, while not annulling its prehistory, did in fact change everything—and Christ did inaugurate a new kingdom. Therefore it is important to see how the New Testament writers, in applying the Old Testament descriptions of the People of God to the Christian community, transformed and not merely transferred the original titles.

A good example is the use made of the Exodus text summarising the Sinai alliance: 'From this you know that now, if you obey my voice and hold fast to my covenant, you of all the nations shall be my very own for all the earth is mine. I will count you a kingdom of priests, a consecrated nation' (*Exod.* 19:5–6).

St Paul writes to Titus: 'He sacrificed himself for us in order to set us free from all wickedness and to purify a people so that it could be his very own and would have no ambition except to do good' (*Tit.* 2:14). It could not be said that God 'sacrificed himself' in order to achieve the exodus; the new demonstration of divine affection infinitely surpasses the old. The freedom of the new Israel is not from tyrannical masters, for they will always be with us, but from 'all wickedness'. The new Israel is to be purified from the multiple preoccupations, political and military, of the original kingdom, and 'have no ambition except to do good'.

The same difference is evident in St Peter's use of the Exodus text: 'But you are a chosen race, a royal priesthood, a consecrated nation, a people set apart to sing the praises of God who called you out of the darkness into his wonderful light. Once you were not a people at all and now you are the People of God; once you were outside the mercy and now you have been given mercy' (1 *Pet.* 2:9–10). Israel sang the praises of God because

> He struck down the first-born of Egypt,
> of man and beast alike,
> he sent signs and wonders
> among you, Egypt,
> against Pharaoh and his officials (*Ps.* 135:8–9).

But we have a purer and a higher motive for praise, because

God has called us 'into his wonderful light'. And, with the same Exodus text in mind, St John writes a hymn to chant our praises to the Saviour:

> You are worthy to take the scroll
> and break the seals of it,
> because you were sacrificed, and with your blood
> you bought men for God
> of every race, language, people and nation
> and made them a line of kings and priests,
> to serve our God and to rule the world (*Rev.* 5:9–10).

Thus the concept of the new People of God is in fact on a considerably higher plane than the Old Testament one. This is what the epistle to the Hebrews argues laboriously in typical Jewish thought-patterns. Both communities are born of a divine alliance, and the greater the alliance the higher the dignity of the People. The epistle argues that the new alliance surpasses the old, because of the superiority of Christ over Moses as mediator, the superiority of Christ's priesthood over that of Aaron, and the superiority of Christ's unique sacrifice over the faint Old Testament foreshadowings. 'And he has entered the sanctuary once and for all, taking with him not the blood of goats and bull calves, but his own blood, having won an eternal redemption for us' (*Heb.* 9:12).

Our function, then, as the new People of God, is to bring to completion and fulfilment all that the Old Testament Israel was meant to do. We do not labour under the same limitations, but it is well to admit that we are exposed to the same dangers, from within and without, that plagued Israel. Nobody was so painfully aware of that, from his own experience as a missionary, as St Paul, and it is good for us to recall his agonising solicitude for the young and new People of God. Luke, in Acts 20, gives a splendid account of Paul's journey from Ephesus to Rome. Paul was depressed, convinced that imprisonment and death awaited him in Jerusalem, and worried about the little Christian communities for which he had worked so hard and suffered so much. On the beach at Miletus he bade a touching farewell to the leaders of the Ephesus community. This speech, which Dupont has called 'the pastoral testament of St Paul', sums up the whole ecclesial theology of the apostolic age, as well as Paul's typically missionary mentality.

> Be on your guard for yourselves and for all the flock of which the Holy Spirit has made you the overseers, to feed the Church of God which he bought with his own blood. I know quite well that when I have gone fierce wolves will invade you and will have no mercy on the flock. Even from your own ranks there will be men coming forward with a travesty of the truth on their lips to induce the disciples to follow them. So be on your guard, remembering how night and day for three years I never failed to keep you right, shedding tears over each one of you. And now I commend you to God, and to the word of his grace that has power to build you up and to give you your inheritance among all the sanctified (*Acts* 20:28–32).

It is a passage that could have been written yesterday.

Has the concept of the Church as the People of God a specific message for the missionary? I think we can, without fear of exaggeration answer, Yes. First, it brings us into direct contact with the fundamental biblical realities on which our outlook must be based, concepts like election, alliance and promise, God's choice, God's appeal, man's reply.

Election involves a divine choice, a divine invitation and a human response. We have been chosen by God, an unmerited free act of divine love to which the only reasonable reaction is one of intense gratitude. This choice is a secret act of the divine will which is externalised and executed by a divine call. As members of the People of God we have been 'called together', convoked into the assembly of the Lord. The aim of a divine call is always to gather, never to scatter. The People of God by its nature denotes unity, not division. So when we talk about the Church scattered among the nations, the Church as 'diaspora', we must remember that the historical Jewish Diaspora was neither a logical development of Israel's history nor an ideal finally attained. It was simply a situation put to use by God as a providential assistance to the infant Church of the apostolic age. The scattered Jewish communities of the Graeco-Roman world helped Paul, as the system of Roman highways helped him, to spread the Good News more quickly and more widely. A People of God in diaspora among the nations is obviously a missionary method, but it should hardly be considered as an end to be desired or a status quo with which we can rest content.

Election and alliance always have a purpose. The Old Testament People of God was called to be a 'kingdom of priests', but priesthood by its nature is an institution for the benefit of others. It is a mediation between God and men, and Israel was destined to be a mediator people. Geographically situated at a crossroads of all the great empires of pre-Christian times, Israel was set up as a link between a God who was universally loving and a humanity pathetically unaware of this. But the missionary dynamism latent in this purpose was so severely restricted by Old Testament conditions that it never found a genuine outlet. We shall see this in more detail later. But this probably accounts for the New Testament desire to show the People of God, not so much as a chosen group, but as a group breaking down all racial barriers. At the first Council of the Church, only twenty years after Christ's death, this statement was made: 'God first arranged to enlist a people for his name out of the pagans' (*Acts.* 15:14). This is a very early, and therefore very precious, indication of how the original Christian community viewed itself and its purpose.

Second, the People of God concept can help to rid us of the contrast, so often unconsciously at the back of our minds, between the Church and the world, which is another way of saying between the Church and humanity. The Church is not, and never was intended to be, an impersonal institution, a giant transmitter relaying instructions to men. The Church is not something to be contrasted with men; it is composed of men, men with all their frailties and fallacies and worries, men struggling, in spite of many distractions and detours, to fight their way to their God. The Church is composed of men who open their hearts to God's call, who respond as best they can to a divine invitation, and who know that they have set out on a road that can lead them to the feet of the Saviour. It is Christ who calls, who beckons forward; it is the Church that responds, aided by his Spirit who dwells within her.

Finally, this concept of the Church can remove some of the obstacles to a fruitful meeting in charity with other religions. The People of God is a simple notion, which all can understand. And it is founded on truths that appeal instinctively to the human spirit—truths like election, divine call, the initiative of God in the whole salvation process, man's free if sometimes hesitant response, a people assembled by God from the four winds, the breath of the Spirit . . . All this creates an atmosphere for dialogue which could not be achieved if we present the Church in terms of a legally defined closed circle, an élite of the self-satisfied. We must not return to the narrow Judaism that Christ encountered and suffered from.

The Pilgrim Church

One paragraph of *Lumen Gentium* puts this theme into words, and does so beautifully: 'While she transcends all limits of time and of race, the Church is destined to extend to all regions of the earth and so to enter into the history of mankind. Moving forward through trial and tribulation, the Church is strengthened by the power of God's grace promised to her by the Lord, so that in the weakness of the flesh she may not waver from perfect fidelity, but remain a bride worthy of her Lord; that moved by the Holy Spirit she may never cease to renew herself, until through the cross she arrives at the light which knows no setting' (*Lum. Gen.* art. 9).

The Church is on pilgrimage, is on the march towards a destination fixed by her Founder. She is therefore moving, alive, dynamic; a very different image indeed from that of a static, monolithic Church, old, wise but weary, a benevolent grandmother ever issuing cautions to boisterous children. She is the crowning act of that long procession in history from the first just man to the last of the saints—and beyond. The Church is in movement, and thus is always becoming, always growing; her future is far more important than her past. Therefore for her members there is no room for complacency, no excuse for standing still; there is still so much to be done. This is a missionary journey, and the destination of the full People of God is still remote.

A pilgrim Church can go forward on her journey only if two conditions are met: support for the road, and a destination at the end of it. Her Founder provided both. The support of the People of God on the march is the promise of divine companionship. 'And know that I am with you always; yes, to the end of time' (*Matt.* 28:20). It is not by accident that this promise occurs as the final phrase in the great missionary mandate, to which we shall return later. And this knowledge that Christ is at his elbow must remain the harassed missionary's greatest consolation—and no sophistry or theological subtlety can take this away from him. Without this, after all, we could neither begin nor continue.

However, the promises to which we anchor our life and work are not merely concerned with the present; they pierce far into the future. They point towards a glorious fulfilment that satisfies the questing human spirit and lifts us above the petty annoyances and reverses of the day. In other words, they are eschatological. The emphasis on eschatology is one of the phenomena of contemporary theology. To those of us who associate the word with the dogmatic tract *De Novissimis*, eschatology is a concept of new and unexpected richness. It is, at heart, the science of Christian hope. And if the just man lives by faith, he certainly works by hope. In our confused, protesting, troubled era, the virtue of hope will be our most secure anchor, the mariner's star that will save us from drifting with wind and tide.

Lumen Gentium devotes articles 48–50 to the eschatological nature of the pilgrim Church. 'However, until there is a new heaven and a new earth where justice dwells, the pilgrim Church in her sacraments and institutions, which pertain to this present time, takes on the appearance of this passing world' (art. 48).

The Church's final destination is a meeting with her returning Lord. In the meantime she shares the tribulations of an imperfect world and a divided humanity. But she must keep before the eyes of all men the destination to which she is trying to lead them. She has been left the enormous task of preparing, day in day out, for the 'universal restoration', of bringing all things under the lordship of Christ. Obviously, this demands, above all else, increasing and urgent missionary activity. Mark 13:10 is perfectly clear: before the Lord's return 'you will stand before governors and kings for my sake, to bear witness before them, since the Good News must first be proclaimed to all the nations'.

In the daily difficulties and frustrations of a missionary's life, nothing can more effectively support him than the conviction that all these contribute to the advance towards a definite goal, that all form a part, no matter how small, of the great plan of God that leads to a final consummation in the kingdom of God. The world and its inhabitants are a strange and often exasperating mixture, and if we do not see them as part of a superbly logical divine plan, they can generate a deep discouragement. The pilgrim Church retains a constant awareness of her messianic character and is thus able to transmit the hope of a glorious consummation and restoration of the world in Christ.

As pilgrim, whether the Church is numerically a little flock or an immense people at any particular moment is not important; what is important is that she marches on. But mere survival is not a march. The Church is on her way to a divinely appointed rendezvous. Neither elated by temporary triumphs nor distressed by opposition she goes on her way, because she is not an invading army but a people humble and poor—a servant and a witness to her Lord. Spectacular victories are not her criterion, but the constant, urgent, earnest witnessing to the truth before the greatest possible number of people.

This is how Christ's kingdom comes; in fact, this is Christ's kingdom. Before Pilate Christ claimed to be king. But what kind of king? Certainly not one according to the traditional image, borrowed from medieval Europe and the more romantic days of merrie England, of a proud figure on a white charger riding forth at the head of a victorious army to conquer an empire—the militant leader of a militant Church. This is not what the New Testament says. Christ, in reply to Pilate, gives a description of his kingship: 'Yes, I am a king. I was born for this, I came into the world for this; to bear witness to the truth; and all who are on the side of truth listen to my voice' (*John* 18:37). Since the kingdom is one of truth, we its citizens are necessarily witnesses to that truth. And as long as truth must be witnessed to, missionaries are needed because this is their speciality. As followers and servants of the King of truth we are dedicated to the full expression and the widest possible diffusion of that truth. As long as there is one who has not heard it we have work to do.

The Church, then, is in continual exodus, on her way from the ancient pre-redemption servitude to the lasting and definitive Promised Land. She moves, as tiny Israel moved, across difficult terrain, dependent on the guiding finger and daily solicitude of her God. The Church is a community that constantly receives and lives on the gift of God—the new and nobler manna of the People of God on the march. As the final stage in God's salvation plan, the Church leads men from Pentecost to the Parousia. Since the Church sets out from Pentecost, she must go forward under the light of the Spirit, the Spirit of truth whose function it is to teach all men all things —and by the aid of this Spirit we must continue to teach all nations . . .

In the light of these basic themes of People of God and pilgrim, the Church emerges as a unity of men in the Spirit—good men, weak men, hesitant men, but essentially men on the move. They are men seeking, questing, experimenting, forging forward through the normal painful human processes of trial and error—pilgrims dust-stained but rejoicing. In view of her destination—the assembly of the human race at the feet of its Saviour—the Church on pilgrimage, the caravan Church in this restless impulsive era, must make many decisions, many choices, shed some of her past rigidity, as she is doing in the liturgy, and renew herself continuously to become all things to all men.

'The Church is also the People of God on its way; it may stop at nothing nor settle anywhere, and its ordinances *ad intra* as well as its limits *ad extra* are always indefinite and sliding. It is also on its way to unity, and it has to realise that every fixation of limits and competences must be provisional, and must never be presented as the eschatological judgement of God, who alone pronounces the final "Come, you blessed" and "Depart from me, you cursed". The moment the Church were to rely completely on its limits and ordinances it would harden in its pilgrim state and thus refuse to submit to God's final judgement' (Fr van Beeck, S.J.).

3 A Church Essentially Missionary

In talking about the essentially missionary nature of the Church the temptation is great, and has already been succumbed to in a few cases, to quote *Lumen Gentium*, articles 13–17, and great expanses of *Ad Gentes*. This serves the laudable purpose of demonstrating beyond doubt that Vatican II was convinced of the urgency and importance of the Church's missionary task, but perhaps here it is better, and less painful, simply to select a few questions and try to give direct answers:

i) What do we mean by the term 'missions'?

ii) Why is the Church essentially missionary?

iii) How does the Church discharge her missionary duty?

i) *What are 'Missions'?*

During the Council debates on the text of *Ad Gentes* there was considerable discussion about the exact meaning of 'missions' and 'missionary'. Can the local clergy of a secularised industrial city in Europe be called missionaries? Can the apostolate in nominally Catholic South America be called missionary work? *Ad Gentes*, article 6, provides the following guidelines: 'Missions is the term usually given to those particular undertakings by which the heralds of the gospel are sent out by the Church and go forth into the whole world to carry out the task of preaching the gospel and planting the Church among peoples or groups who do not yet believe in Christ ... The

33

specific purpose of this missionary activity is evangelisation and the planting of the Church among those peoples and groups where she has not yet taken root.'

It is important to notice the precise limits imposed by this definition: 'peoples and groups where she has not yet taken root'. In the years before the Council a certain confusion about the meaning of missionary work was prevalent in most of Europe. The chief reason for this was that the French word 'mission' has a wider meaning than our word 'missions'. It can refer equally to missionary work proper and to the apostolate among the de-Christianised masses in Europe. When the Church in Europe realised the tragic scale of the 'apostasy of the masses' there was a clarion-call to 'missionary activity' but exclusively in terms of the urgent local European problem. This did not help the cause of missions in the strict sense, because obviously if the needs of the local Church were so urgent then it would be a lack of Christian charity to abandon the 'mission field' of one's own diocese and emigrate to plant the Church elsewhere.

Still more confusion was caused by the call for 'missionaries' to South America, the urgency of whose situation nobody denies. But is it a missionary area according to the traditional terminology of four centuries of Church history and according to the description of *Ad Gentes*? Even strictly in terms of need, have the proponents of the new and wider meaning of mission always presented the full facts? In a sharp attack on this trend, Fr Eugene Hillman, C.S.Sp., in *The Church as Mission*, mentions that 'in France alone there are more priests and sisters than there are in the whole of Asia and Africa together. Even Latin America has a general ratio of one priest for every five thousand souls, as compared with one to seventeen thousand in Africa, and one to eighty thousand in Asia.' Using statistics published in 1961 he continues: 'There are more than five thousand priests in French schools, for the most part teaching merely secular subjects. One school alone in Brussels has on its faculty more priests than the entire city of Leopoldville in the Congo; and there are seminaries in Switzerland with an average of one priest for every two students.' And he concludes that if we accept this wider conception of missions the situation is almost certain to get worse, because then 'the Church's pastoral functions, home missions, social action, university students, workers, poor peasants, blind intellectuals, old folks, orphans, etc., may all be regarded as the proper objects of "missionary activity".'

Thus it is vital to make the necessary distinctions between two different functions of the Church: the care of the faithful already within the visible Church established in their own country, and the act of assembling a Christian community which does not yet exist or is just struggling to find its feet. In keeping the distinction clear we have no desire to set these two activities against one another; both are necessary, but to confuse them is ultimately to do harm to both. Again to quote Fr Hillman: 'No matter what words we may use, one thing is certain. Both the pastoral and the missionary functions of the Church are equally essential to the life of the whole Church everywhere; and the mission of the Church is not being served where one or the other of these activities is being neglected in practice. Where the apostolic zeal of the Christian community —whether in Europe, the Americas, Asia, Africa, or Oceania —is primarily turned inward, defensively on itself, and not equally turned outward in a truly catholic attitude of world-wide dimensions, there the faith is bound to wither and to die.'

However, missionary work is not restricted exclusively to a search for pagans in some remote bush village. Again, let us take our point of departure from *Ad Gentes*, article 6: 'In this missionary activity of the Church various stages are sometimes found side by side: first, that of the beginning or planting, then that of newness or youth. When these stages have passed, the

Church's missionary activity does not cease. Rather, there lies upon the particular Churches which are already set up the duty of continuing this activity and of preaching the gospel to those still outside.'

Chapter 2 of *Ad Gentes* describes the three stages or degrees of missionary activity that can normally be distinguished, even though not always given the same titles.

a) The pre-kerygmatic stage—the missionary's witness to Christ by the example of Christian living and the practical demonstration of the charity of Christ. This is normally the first contact between the Church and a human group, and in many cases explicit preaching of the gospel is not immediately possible. This makes it more urgent that the missionary, through his own faith, conviction and charity, tell forth the attractiveness of the Christian life, and take an active and intelligent interest in the complete development of the people among whom he lives.

b) The kerygmatic stage—the first preaching, the 'kerygma' as the New Testament understands it, evangelisation in the original sense of that term. This verbal proclamation aims at leading a group to explicit faith in Christ by means of a period of catechumenate, and reaches its terminus in the reception of baptism. This is the heart of all missionary activity—proclaiming the name of Christ and his death and resurrection, so that an audience 'may believe and be freely converted to the Lord, and may sincerely cling to him', as *Ad Gentes*, article 13, puts it. This article 13 must surely be the most scripturally orientated article of all the Council documents: there are twenty-seven New Testament references in the opening two sentences.

c) The stage known as the 'planting' of the Church, or the formation of a Christian community. This is achieved by the administration of the sacraments, instruction in the basic themes of faith, the gradual formation of the new Christians in the values, ideals and morals of the gospel, and the promotion of a realistic liturgical life in the young community. Thus, while evangelisation proper is concerned mainly with the formation of the individual Christian, the third stage deals with the formation of communities. And it reaches its culmination in the erection of the local hierarchy with indigenous clergy, and thus in the establishment of a new 'local church'.

Only at this stage is the local church able to fulfil its function of Christianising society, of deepening and expanding the Christian life. This is by no means an unnecessary flourish added to missionary work. As long as the Christian communities in any country do not express themselves through the native elements of that country—its language, customs, art—they retain a foreign character. This makes their existence precarious, and hardly realises fully the idea of planting and taking root. The generality of men cannot long remain true to the Church in surroundings that are either indifferent or actively hostile. Also, a genuinely planted, mature local church will prove its coming of age by its own missionary spirit and activity. But we must help young churches to develop this spirit and put it into practical effect.

Clearly, these differing stages of apostolic activity are not intended to be sharply separated by strict lines of demarcation; they fade naturally into one another, and in many cases aspects of all three will be found simultaneously. One cannot determine with mathematical precision when any or all of them come to an end; a young church arrives at maturity by a process of natural growth—and this is always slow. But all three stages are genuinely missionary work, because all are directed towards the establishment of a mature, self-sufficient local church.

(ii) *Why is the Church Essentially Missionary?*

The Church has, from her foundation and by her nature, a mission to all men. This follows from three facts:

the desire of God, clearly expressed in Scripture, to save
all men without exception;
Christ's explicit command to carry the Good News to
every nation;
the Church's obligation to give glory to God by leading
all men to his knowledge and love.

The universal salvific will of God is a truth of faith explicit in
the Bible and repeatedly emphasised by the teaching Church.
From this it follows that any man, or any community of men,
that wishes to accept and fulfil the will of God is automatically
orientated towards the universality of salvation—towards a
diffusion of God to all men. This must form an integral part of
the interior motivation, the attitude of mind, of every Christian.

This universal salvific will is implied in the idea of creation.
By creation a contact is established between God and the
individual man. Man is created by a loving God, and for a
loving God. As creature, man is not an end in himself; his life
is not its own purpose. Man by his nature stretches out to his
Maker. A Godward movement is as much part of man as is
physical locomotion. But in which direction does man look to
find his God: does he gaze towards the rising sun, or take his
troubles to a local shrine, or pin his faith in a Welfare State, or
seek his happiness in a narcissist self-sufficiency? Men's gods may
be many, but men's Creator is one. It is our privilege, and therefore our duty, to tell them so.

As a rational being, only man has the capacity to know and to
love. These are noble attributes, and they need a noble object on
which to focus. We marvel, and justly, at the disciplined and
co-ordinated use of intellect that enables men to reach the moon,
but for man's inner spirit the moon is as unrewarding as the
earth. Only God can satisfy man.

Historically, the divine will has been progressively unveiled
through the three stages of salvation history as the Bible records

them: the Old Testament—God's benign activity through his people Israel; the gospels—God active through the person of his Son; the rest of the New Testament writings—describing God at work in the world through his Church. And at each of these stages God's salvific will for all reveals itself in a new way. In the Old Testament Israel finally came to know that God loved all men, not merely the sons of Abraham. Christ died to redeem all men—the universal divine love in action. After his resurrection he left to his apostles the command to tell the story of redemption to all without exception.

As we shall see, God's universal concern for mankind was always accepted, in theory and in a vague manner, by the Israelites. But they never felt the necessity to draw practical missionary conclusions from this; in fact, only towards the end of the prophetic period did they begin to state it clearly. One of the strongest expressions of God's love for all his creatures occurs in the book of Wisdom, the last book of the Old Testament to be written, and obviously by a hellenised Jew.

> Yes, you love all that exists, you hold nothing of what you have made in abhorrence,
> for had you hated anything, you would not have formed it.
> And how, had you not willed it, could a thing persist,
> how be conserved if not called forth by you?
> You spare all things because all things are yours, Lord, lover of life,
> you whose imperishable spirit is in all.
> Little by little, therefore, you correct those who offend,
> you admonish and remind them of how they have sinned,
> so that they may abstain from evil and trust in you, Lord
> (*Wis.* 11: 24—12:2).

The great proof of God's universal love was, of course, the redemption. Christ's task was to demonstrate, beyond all shadow of doubt, the limitless affection of his Father for all men. He witnessed to this universality all his life, but witnessed to it supremely by his death. His death not merely proved his Father's desire to save all; it did in fact save all, because it bought them back into the union with God that had been sundered by sin. Not merely did the redemption reveal divine love; it objectively achieved the aim of divine love—universal salvation. All that remained to be done in the 'last days' of the salvation plan was that the historical truth of the redemption be presented to every man so that he could understand God's love and respond with his own. This is what St Paul is saying in the classic passage to Timothy urging prayers for all men, pagans and persecutors included.

> My advice is that, first of all, there should be prayers offered for everyone—petitions, intercessions and thanksgiving—and especially for kings and others in authority, so that we may be able to live religious and reverent lives in peace and quiet. To do this is right, and will please God our saviour: he wants everyone to be saved and reach full knowledge of the truth. For there is only one God, and there is only one mediator between God and mankind, himself a man, Christ Jesus, who sacrificed himself as a ransom for them all. He is the evidence of this, sent at the appointed time, and I have been named a herald and apostle of it and—I am telling the truth and no lie—a teacher of the faith and the truth to the pagans. In every place, then, I want the men to lift their hands up reverently in prayer, with no anger or argument (1 *Tim.* 2:1–8).

It seems obvious that the universality of God's love demands and deserves an equal universality of response. And, in general, men attempt to respond, but in a pathetically bewildering variety of ways, some partially true, some transparently wide of the mark. This being the case, is God's salvific will being thwarted? There is a grave dilemma here at which we must look more closely in talking about the relationship between Church and salvation. Here it is sufficient to say that human freedom is one of the postulates of the divine plan. Having made man free, God scrupulously respects his freedom. Besides, God, in his scheme of salvation, normally works on the hearts of men by the apparent accidents of history and geography and by their contacts with other men. The supreme form of contact, explicit and organised, is missionary activity, which is, in the last analysis, nothing more or less than God giving visible proof in action of his desire to draw all men to himself. As Fr Adrian Hastings has written: 'Missionary activity is in a special way the sacrament of the universality of God's love.' *Ad Gentes*, article 9, says the same thing more forcefully: 'Missionary activity is nothing else and nothing less than a manifestation or epiphany of God's will, and the fulfilment of that will in the world and in world history.'

Next, the Church is by her nature missionary because she must obey her Founder's express command to teach all men. Even if there were no incarnation, from what we know of God on the Old Testament evidence alone we should have to presume some form of missionary activity. But because of what the incarnation was and what it did, evangelisation is the very life-blood of the People of God. We can be grateful that Vatican II buried—we hope forever—the attitude that missionary work was a fringe activity of a strongly established Church, a pious cause that might be attended to when the home fires were first brightly burning. How, in view of the biblical evidence, such an idea could have persisted in the minds of even the best of men is difficult to understand. One of the key contributions of *Lumen Gentium* is to affirm, clearly and strongly, that missionary activity is at the very heart of the Church; it is not an optional extra or a work of devotional supererogation.

Because the Church relays the voice of Christ to men, she must transmit his whole message, entire and pure. And she cannot for a moment forget that his parting words were: 'Go out to the whole world.' This universal mission given by Christ to his Church is placed by the evangelists in the final section of the gospel—the period between resurrection and ascension. This can be called the 'ecclesial' section of the gospel narratives, when the machinery of the Church is being set in motion—sacraments, preaching, mission. And over all this section sounds, loud and clear, the command that knows no limits of space or nation or time: 'Proclaim the Good News to all creation.'

To be true to herself, the Church must be unflinchingly true to her Master and Founder. And in this she can have no rest, no stopping half-way; as long as there are men on the earth, she must engage in every attempt possible to bring them the Good News. '. . . so am I sending you'—the very word 'send' means mission, and so the whole Church is on mission, and cannot be otherwise. The New Testament guide-lines for ecclesial activity are vague in some details, reasonably explicit in others—but there is no room for doubt as far as missions are concerned. Missionary activity is not so much the work of the Church as simply the Church at work.

Third, the Church is essentially missionary because of the obligation laid on her to give glory to God by leading all men to his knowledge and love. It is interesting, in an abstract academic way, to speculate on world, men, salvation, and their inter-relations and fate if the incarnation had not taken place. But this is the kind of intellectual crossword puzzle for which there is no prize. Christ has come into the world, he has died to save us and risen to glorify us, and history, world and men can never be the same again. The redemption is a piece of information so tremendous, and with such profound effects on the lives of men, that we must set out at once to bring it to them.

The human life that encounters no knowledge of God's love is a blighted, stunted life, no matter what else may fill it.

'By manifesting Christ, the Church reveals to men the real truth about their condition and their total vocation. For Christ is the source and model of that renewed humanity, penetrated with brotherly love, sincerity, and a peaceful spirit, to which all aspire' (Ad Gentes, art. 8). The incarnation, God's supreme intervention in history, is the central act and fact of the human story. It strains outward to be known; it is the food of all the hungry ones of the earth. Is it a sentimental exaggeration to say that the greatest crime against humanity is to keep from it the nourishment that Christ died to give? This would be a denial of the very purpose of the incarnation; instead of bringing light to the nations this would be concealing the truth from those who cry out for it, depriving the hungry of 'their allowance of food at the proper time'. Surely this is a form of the 'eternal sin' against the holy Spirit that is not forgiven. 'The people's curse is on the man who hoards the wheat, a blessing on him who sells it' (Prov. 11:26).

Thus, both the love of God for men and the love of men for their fellows demand that we share with all men, and to the fullest possible extent, the great news of redemption, the only genuine Good News there is. We are blessed to have received it, and twice blessed when we are generous in giving it, in sharing it with all. Missionary activity follows from the incarnation as naturally as light flows from the sun.

The image of light and sun leads us back to the concept of giving glory to God. 'Finally, by means of this missionary activity, God is fully glorified, provided that men consciously and fully accept his work of salvation, which he has accomplished in Christ' (Ad Gentes, art. 7). But what exactly is the meaning of that deceptively simple statement: 'God is glorified'?

In the Old Testament the 'glory of Yahweh' connotes two related ideas: his infinite greatness (the Hebrew word translated 'glory' refers to the real value of a thing, not to an external attribute); and the dynamic interventions by which he revealed his greatness. Thus the Israelites made contact with the glory of the Lord through the manna in the desert (*Exod.* 16:4–7), through thunder and tempest (*Ps.* 29), through awesome theophanies (*Deut.* 5:23–25), and through the splendour of the temple ceremonial (1 Kings 8:10–13).

With the coming of the Messiah, theophanies and temple faded into the shadows. As Son of God, the Messiah was 'the radiant light of God's glory and the perfect copy of his nature' (*Heb.* 1:3); he was, in fact, 'the Lord of Glory' (1 *Cor.* 2:8). These titles echo the two Old Testament aspects of 'glory': Christ was really God, equal in greatness and majesty with the Father; Christ revealed God to man. He gave glory to his Father by presenting to men the divine goodness in all its beauty.

This is the function that the Church must perpetuate—holding up to the gaze of all men the infinite attractiveness and lovableness of her Lord. In doing this, she glorifies God in the full biblical meaning of the phrase. Men give their response when they see, accept, acknowledge and worship God's greatness and kindness. This is how they glorify God. 'Giving glory to God' is a rather clumsy phrase which suggests, erroneously, that men add something to God. There is nothing that can be added to his infinity, but men do add a new dimension to their own lives when they believe and rejoice in the glory of their God. Then they share in some of this glory; they too 'shine in the world like bright stars', as Paul says (*Phil.* 2:15). To give glory to God means to acknowledge and praise his love, and to radiate this discovery joyfully.

From all this it is obvious that the glory of God is the chief aim of missionary activity: to tell all men of God's goodness and lead them to believe in it, to live by it, and to adore. It is enlightening to notice how many of the innumerable scriptural references to the glory of God occur in what can only be described as a missionary context. This is true even in the Old Testament; the final section of the book of Isaiah contains two splendid examples.

> Above you Yahweh now rises
> and above you his glory appears.
> The nations come to your light
> and kings to your dawning brightness (*Is.* 60:2–3).

> I am coming to gather the nations of every language. They shall come to witness my glory. I will give them a sign and send some of their survivors to the nations ... to the distant islands that have never heard of me or seen my glory. They will proclaim my glory to the nations (*Is.* 66:18–19).

The New Testament makes the connection between the glory of God and the spread of the Good News much more explicit. At Christ's birth, angels carried the news of what had happened in nearby Bethlehem to a few astonished shepherds, 'and the glory of the Lord shone around them' (*Luke* 2:9). At Cana Christ took compassion on a young couple and their harassed caterer, and John remarks: 'He let his glory be seen, and his disciples believed in him' (*John* 2:12). In making the raising of Lazarus a test of faith, Jesus asks: 'Have I not told you that if you believe you will see the glory of God?' (*John* 11:40). The glory of both Father and Son is expressly linked to man's salvation in John's Last Supper compendium of Christ's remarks: 'Father, the hour has come: glorify your Son so that your Son may glorify you; and through the power over all mankind that you have given him, let him give eternal life to all those you have entrusted to him' (*John* 17:1–2).

As we might expect, Paul is forever reminding his Christians of the glory of God. After all, he had been blinded by it on his way to Damascus. The full range of Paul's fire, charity and apostolic experience fuses in the magnificent hymn to God's glory and man's salvation that we find in the opening verses of the epistle to the Ephesians.

> Blessed be God the Father of our Lord Jesus Christ,
> who has blessed us with all the spiritual blessings of heaven in Christ.
> Before the world was made, he chose us, chose us in Christ, to be holy and spotless, and to live through love in his presence,
> determining that we should become his adopted sons, through Jesus Christ
> for his own kind purposes,
> to make us praise the glory of his grace ... (*Eph.* 1:3–6).

God's salvific will is both universal and eternal—'before the world was made'; its revelation and accomplishment through Christ demand that we 'praise the glory of his grace'. And these words are not confined to a small select group. This long hymn to God's salvation plan takes the literary form of a series of six blessings, and the final one is directed to the pagans, who, by their acceptance of God's glory, now form part of the Ephesus community.

> Now you too, in him,
> have heard the message of the truth and the good news of your salvation,
> and have believed it;
> and you too have been stamped with the seal of the Holy Spirit of the Promise,
> the pledge of our inheritance
> which brings freedom for those whom God has taken for his own, to make his glory praised (*Eph.* 1:13–14).

It is not surprising, then, that the splendid eschatological vision of John should see all creation chanting in eternity the glory o God—Creator, Redeemer and Lord: 'Then I heard all the living things in creation—everything that lives in the air, and on the ground, and under the ground, and in the sea, crying, "To the One who is sitting on the throne and to the Lamb, be all praise, honour, glory and power, for ever and ever"' (*Rev.* 5:13).

From the theological viewpoint, it is particularly consoling to notice how *Ad Gentes* sets the Church's missionary work firmly in the heart of the fundamental Christian mystery of the Trinity. The love of the Father, the incarnation of his Son and the sending of his Spirit, provide the origin, the *raison d'être* and the motive force of all missionary activity. Mission, in every sense of the word, comes from the Father, the Beginning who knows no beginning, the origin of all activity—and must inevitably return to him. It finds its supreme expression in the Son, who by his redemptive and transforming incarnation founded a visible agency of salvation—the Church. The Church in turn is supported, guided and urged onwards by the Spirit, who brings light to the darkness of mystery and testimony to the depths of divine love. Here it is worth re-reading the opening articles of chapter 1 of *Ad Gentes*: article 2—'the decree of God the Father'; article 3—'Jesus Christ was sent into the world'; article 4—'Christ sent the holy Spirit from the Father'. From this it is not only logical but inevitable that article 5 should conclude: 'Since then the duty has weighed upon the Church to spread the faith and the saving work of Christ.' As Fr Amalorpavadass says: 'The love overflowing from the Trinitarian fellowship and made visible in Christ must reach all men through the living testimony of all Church members, a testimony which is at the same time an invitation to communion. The Church's mission is thus an uninterrupted flow from the "Fountain of love" which has its highest source in God the Father.'

What all this means in effect is that apostolic activity has been re-directed to its true terminus, Christ; it is Christ-centred rather than Church-centred. We now have a clearer vision of mission as an activity dominated and determined by Christ— springing from his redemptive act and applying its fruits to men. The great missionaries of former times may have understood this better than we do; the undivided love of Christ rather than speculation about the nature of the Church drove them to the ends of the earth. And Paul is proud to say that the irresistible incentive of his apostolate was that 'the love of Christ overwhelms us' (2 *Cor.* 5:14).

Thus, the glory of God, the command of Christ and the good of men all converge on the single conclusion: 'As the salt of the earth and the light of the world, the Church is summoned with special urgency to save and renew every creature' (*Ad Gentes*, art. 1). Again to quote Fr Amalorpavadass: 'Thus, missionary activity is one of the "innermost requirements" of the Church's catholicity and of the power of life and growth contained in Love itself. This motive is strengthened, first by the command of Christ; second, by the realisation that human weakness and wickedness make it imperative for one who loves, to offer to all men the helps to salvation which are at work in the Church; third, by the conviction that the best way to reveal man to himself is to reveal Christ to him; fourth, the need to purify and to restore to Christ all that is truth and grace in non-Christian religions; finally, that God may be fully glorified by the full accomplishment of his plan for men's salvation in Christ.'

It is worth pointing out that the reasons for missionary activity that we have been considering in this chapter are in no way weakened by the gloomy predictions of the statisticians. It is true that the Church is still a minority on the earth, and that mankind grows in number more quickly than Christian communities can. But two comments must be made.

One of the finest attributes of the human spirit is its constant endeavour to surmount difficulties rather than weep over them. If St Paul had been satisfied to have the Church remain a little flock in Jerusalem and Antioch, he would not have undertaken the conversion of the Roman empire. Has the light of the holy Spirit grown dimmer since then? Has the gospel lost its power to attract and transform men? The only valid conclusion to be drawn from the Church's present situation is that we, as missionaries, have even more to do than ever before, because the will of God is perfectly clear from the whole biblical message, and we must continue to labour towards the goal of 'one Lord, one faith, one baptism' (*Eph.* 4:5). It is our privilege to tell men how much God loves them, and, irrespective of men's reactions, the glory of the Father, the will of Christ and our own charity oblige us to proclaim this by word and deed. We are a messianic community, which means that we are sent by God as his messengers to men. And surely he tells us, as he told a shattered Israel in exile:

do not be afraid, for I am with you;
stop being anxious and watchful, for I am your God.
I give you strength, I bring you help,
I uphold you with my victorious right hand (*Is.* 41:10).

And does not our faintheartedness merit the gentle reproach given once to braver men: 'Why are you so frightened, you men of little faith?'

It is unsound exegesis to take refuge in the Old Testament idea of the 'remnant', or in Christ's title of 'little flock'—'There is no need to be afraid, little flock, for it has pleased your Father to give you the kingdom' (*Luke* 12:32). From the context—the Father's care for the poor—it seems clear that Christ is referring to the humility and poverty of spirit of his followers, not to their numerical strength. And the remnant of Israel, the 'survivors', was a temporary condition of the People of God, part of the historical 'narrowing-down' process which reached its culmination in the person of Christ. But his coming changed the face of the earth, and 'opened the door of faith to the pagans', as Paul quickly saw (*Acts* 14:27). It is vital to remember that the Jewish mentality at the end of the Old Testament period was that of a tiny community clustered around the Jerusalem temple, fearful of the new empires of Greece and Rome that seemed poised to swallow it up. The young communities of Paul saw themselves and the world quite differently. They suffered from no ghetto complex; rather, filled with the courage of Pentecost and the charity of Christ, they knew that their duty was to spread the Good News, to run to the frontiers of the known world as envoys of the Lord of all. Like them, we can take as our motto the realistic but intensely encouraging words of Christ: 'In the world you will have trouble, but be brave: I have conquered the world' (*John* 16:33).

iii) *How does the Church Discharge her Missionary Duty?*

Ad Gentes, in answering this question, mentions three distinct organisms:

a) The College of Bishops, on which 'the responsibility to proclaim the gospel throughout the world falls primarily'. Therefore the Synod of Bishops 'should give special consideration to missionary activity' (*Ad Gentes*, art. 29).

b) The Congregation for the Evangelisation of Peoples, which is described as the only one competent curial office for all missions and for the whole of missionary activity. 'This office should direct and co-ordinate missionary work itself as well as missionary co-operation throughout the world' (*Ad Gentes*, art. 29).

c) The missionary institutes, 'which take as their own special task that duty of preaching the gospel which weighs upon the whole Church . . . Sent by legitimate authority, they go out faithfully and obediently to those who are far from Christ. They are set apart for the work to which they have been called as ministers of the gospel' (*Ad Gentes*, art. 23).

Vatican II, however, did not spell out in detail the relations between these three organisms; it could scarcely have done so. In the universal aggiornamento and renewal since *Ad Gentes* was issued, how have they attempted to come to grips with their tasks?

In terms of the universal Church, the ultimate responsibility for preaching the gospel has been placed squarely on the College of Bishops. This is simply an application of the principle of episcopal collegiality—the co-responsibility of the bishops with the Pope for all the Church's manifold operations. Since missionary activity is a special sphere, and a highly practical one, it is obvious that the College, or even the Synod of Bishops, can deal with it only in a very general manner. It has yet to be seen to what extent the Synod wishes to do so.

Much more to the point is the role of the national episcopal conferences of the mission-sending countries. Again, their responsibilities are stated clearly: 'As members of the body of bishops, which succeeds the College of Apostles, all bishops are consecrated not just for some one diocese, but for the salvation of the entire world . . . In his own diocese, with which he comprises a single unit, the bishop stimulates, promotes, and directs the work for the missions . . . In order that the missionary activity of individual bishops on behalf of the whole Church may be expressed more effectively, it will be helpful for Episcopal Conferences to regulate those affairs which concern the orderly co-operation of their own region' (*Ad Gentes*, art. 38).

These are grave responsibilities, for which many episcopal conferences were quite unprepared. Traditionally, many bishops have been content to allow the Congregation for the Evangelisation of Peoples and the missionary institutes to look after missionary activity, and felt that they had discharged their own duty adequately by allowing some institutes a certain degree of freedom to seek vocations and support. *Ad Gentes*, articles 28–39, offers, both to episcopal conferences and to individual bishops, several suggestions for stirring up a truly missionary life and spirit among their priests and people. But it would be unrealistic to expect that bishops, already severely burdened by the pastoral care and administration of their own dioceses, should overnight give priority to missionary needs. The development of a dynamic missionary spirit in the home dioceses will take time, and can only come about through much closer contacts with missionary institutes and with missionaries themselves.

The Congregation for the Evangelisation of Peoples received more from the Council than a new name. Rather severely criticised before and during Vatican II as over-centralised and out of touch with the practical problems, the Congregation has taken several initiatives towards renewal. As a curial office, it is concerned chiefly with administration, but administration of an enterprise truly world-wide, with all the variety of situations and circumstances which that involves. This should normally demand an international staff at the Congregation headquarters —an ideal not yet realised. But the Congregation has taken two steps in that direction: increasing to over seventy the number of its consultors; instituting the 'Council of 24', composed of twelve bishops from mission territories (five from Asia, five from Africa, two from Oceania), four bishops from mission-sending countries, four Superiors General of missionary institutes, and four representatives of Pontifical Mission Works. This Council is not merely a consultative body—its members take part in the plenary meetings of the Congregation with full voting rights.

When we come to the actual contact of the Church with mission countries, we find that this is achieved almost exclusively through the missionary institutes. This has been the case since the beginning of the nineteenth century, and their continued existence was automatically accepted as necessary until our own day. Now, some claim that these institutes, though they may have a glorious past, certainly have no future, that they belong to a vanished era of missionary endeavour, and that they no longer find a place in the new missionary perspectives of Vatican II.

It is not difficult to show that this is untrue. A brief look at the spiritual basis, history and nature of missionary institutes demonstrates that they still form an eminently suitable agency through which the Church can exercise her apostolate to the nations. These remarks refer especially to exclusively missionary institutes, but apply to all institutes that accept missions as a distinct activity and train their members accordingly.

Spiritual basis: All Christian life is based on an imitation of Christ. But for the members of a missionary institute this imitation of Christ is specified by a particular viewpoint. It is an imitation of Christ the Saviour, Christ the Preacher, Christ the Teacher, Christ the Healer, Christ the Public Witness to his Father. Their religious life is a service of Christ in his members. Not for them the silence of the cloister, but, by deliberate choice, the heat, dust and clamour of the market-place. This, of course, is true of all forms of the active apostolate, but it is true in a particular way of missionaries. The reason is that missionaries express their love for God, not merely by loving his children, but by loving and actively serving the most needy of his children—those who have never heard of him or know least about him.

History: The historical evolution of missionary societies is illuminating. Since 1622, direct responsibility for the mission to the unevangelised has been assigned to the Congregation for the Propagation of the Faith, to use its old title. Before the establishment of the Congregation there were no missionary institutes in the Church, and missionary work was done by members of religious orders not founded specifically for that work. The first Society to be exclusively missionary was born of the conviction of a French Jesuit, Fr de Rhodes, that the precise nature of the mission to the unevangelised was not understood by many missionaries, and that steps were not being taken by bishops on the missions to form indigenous churches. As a result of his complaints, the Congregation, in 1658, appointed three French secular priests as Vicars Apostolic to territories in the Far East, with orders to take immediate measures to form an indigenous clergy. They needed missionaries from France, and a house for the recruiting of priest-volunteers was opened in Paris. This was the beginning of the first specifically missionary institute in the Church—the Paris Foreign Missions Society.

Missionary institutes, then, were born of the Church's increasing awareness and appreciation of the nature and demands of true mission work. And as this awareness grew over the past 150 years, more and more exclusively missionary institutes appeared.

Nature: By their community structure and their singleness of aim, missionary institutes seem particularly suited to the Church's present mammoth missionary task. It is evident that successful apostolic effort over a prolonged period demands a considerable degree of continuity of method. This is possible only through a continuity of personnel. But the concept of continuity involves the concept of organisation, and, in the present context, of community. The heroic isolated efforts of missionaries like St Francis Xavier and St Peter Claver are certainly worthy of admiration, but are no longer capable of imitation. Even in the primitive situation described in the New Testament writings, the lone work of Paul quickly gave way to a group activity, as is clear from the growing list of 'fellow workers in Christ Jesus' mentioned in his letters, for example in Romans 16. Only an organised community with missions as a common aim can provide the continuity that is necessary for successful missionary activity in all its stages. This is recognised quite plainly in *Ad Gentes*, article 27—an admirable conciliar compliment to all missionary institutes: 'For many centuries now, these communities have borne the burden of the day and the heat, devoting themselves to missionary labour either entirely or in part. Often, vast territories were committed to them by the Holy See for evangelisation, and there they gathered together a new people for God, a local Church loyal to its own shepherds. These communities have founded Churches by their own sweat, and even their blood. In the future they will serve these Churches with their zeal and experience in a spirit of brotherly co-operation.'

This is the age of specialisation. Naturally, then, the current emphasis is on institutions devoted to a particular sphere of activity—teaching, nursing, social work. An institute whose total resources and training are directed to missions seems the only business-like way of coming to grips with mission problems. The contemporary secular world sets high value on technique and efficiency. Only a specialist missionary society can undertake to train members in specific missionary techniques, and thereby achieve maximum efficiency from the manpower available.

In the current clamour for specialists, it is well to point out that the missionary is, by his calling and training, a specialist also. By his skill in presenting the message of Christ, his adaptation to a new culture and milieu, his priestly ministry in a non-Christian environment, his personal apostolic experience and the traditions of his institute, he performs a specialist task, and gives to a human community a service for which there is no substitute.

Therefore there seems no reason to fear that missionary institutes are at the end of their day. And we must ask bluntly: if they do not continue to go out to the nations, who will go? We should take warning from the experiences of the past. In

1952 Pius XII pleaded, with extreme and moving urgency, for more priests for Africa. The response to his appeal in the encyclical *Fidei Donum* was, to put it mildly, disappointing; in 1964 it was calculated that only about 300 priests had gone to Africa as a result of *Fidei Donum*. Again, we must not be lulled into an illusion of security by the fact that every Christian is a missionary. This is true: 'The obligation of spreading the faith is imposed on every disciple of Christ, according to his ability' (*Lumen Gentium*, art. 17). But so very few can actively and personally engage in mission work itself, and thus the missionary remains, and must remain, the indispensable channel of Christ's contact with men who do not yet know him. Without the missionary, and without the institute which trains and supports him, the Church's missionary movement is paralysed at its source. In a word, missionary institutes are still an efficacious response to Christ's command and the Church's duty to bring the good news of salvation to all men.

Of course, these institutes cannot, and should not try to, take shelter from the present wind of change. Certainly there will be changes—in the institutes themselves, in their methods of recruitment and training, in their relations with one another and with the episcopal conferences of both the home and the mission countries. One of the most urgent problems, from the point of view of both Church and institutes, is to find the ideal relationship between the institutes and their local churches of origin. The institutes go forth on their apostolate on behalf of the universal Church; they represent the universal character and vocation of the Church, and normally this is clear from their spirit and their international structure. But how can such institutes represent, with equal clarity, the missionary function of the local European churches from which their members come?

It has been suggested that their international character is an obstacle in this case. However, for an international institute to renounce its international character would be, in the contemporary context, an absurdity. Nations are moving closer together, and organisations that began by being national strive to become international. And it is easy for a purely national group to be suspected of an insidious neo-colonialism; it is sufficient to recall some of the accusations that sections of the 'third world' have levelled, unjustly, at national charitable agencies like the German Misereor and the American Catholic Relief Service.

The solution, then, seems to lie in the area of closer and more clearly defined contacts between the institutes and the bishops of their members' dioceses of origin. It seems a pity, for example, that a missionary, in order to become a member of an institute, should have to withdraw canonically from his own diocese, and return home from his missionary work only to find himself a stranger, an outsider, having little in common with his brother-priests in the pastoral ministry. Is there no way by which missionaries can come 'in from the cold'? Surely it would be better, more Christian, more in the spirit of Vatican II, more in harmony with all 'the signs of the times', if a missionary were to go out as a representative of his diocese, incarnating in a mission territory the missionary ideals and duties of his diocese. Both bishops and institutes will have to seize whatever opportunities are available to approach this ideal—incardination of missionaries in their diocese of origin, collaboration in awakening genuine and intelligent interest in missions, common recruitment of vocations, common training, at least for part of the course, of students for the missionary and the secular priesthood. In short, we must all try harder to find a way by which missionaries can take their true place in the Church, not on the periphery but at the heart, and insert themselves completely, with full confidence, in the local church that gave them their initial missionary impulse by baptism and confirmation.

However, in all this, missionary institutes must be given

rights that correspond in some way to their grave duties. They should not be expected to renounce their true function, sink their identity and struggle desperately for survival in the present extremely difficult vocations climate. Co-operation rather than competition should mark the relations between diocesan and missionary priests in their approach to the faithful of the home dioceses, who have always shown themselves so generous and magnanimous to all who carry Christ's message.

These are practical problems to which answers must be found as soon as possible. The fundamental postulate for an equitable solution will remain the great insight of Vatican II—that the Church, to be true to herself, must be on mission. Mission is a supernatural reality, and as such has God for alpha and omega. Without missionary activity the Church could not realise her cardinal characteristics, because she would be neither catholic nor permanent. The Church lives by charity, and the offering of truth to all men is still the highest form of supernatural charity. If the Church were to cease exercising this charity to men, which is impossible, she would have tolled her own death-knell.

4 Missions—An Old Testament Ideal

Since a universal mission is so prominent a characteristic of the new People of God, we are justified in searching for some foreshadowing of it in the Old Testament. We have already said that Israel was constituted by God as a witnessing and a mediating people, and these attributes would seem to demand some activity outwards to the rest of the world somewhat akin to our missionary apostolate. However, we search in vain in the pages of the Old Testament for any record of Israelite 'evangelisation'. Essentially, Israel had sufficient knowledge of God and of the God-man relationship to enable her to communicate both valuable theological information and more elevated ethical standards to her pagan neighbours. The Israelites accepted the oneness of God as a basic tenet of their faith; in fact their monotheism must have seemed nothing short of fanatical to their more liberal oriental contemporaries. This one God was the God of all men, but yet, apart from Israel, men groped in vain to find him. Only Israel knew him, because he had shown himself to her in theophany, prophecy and prodigy. Deutero-Isaiah put all this into words:

> There is no other god besides me,
> a God of integrity and a saviour;
> there is none apart from me.
> Turn to me and be saved,
> all the ends of the earth,
> for I am God unrivalled (*Is.* 45:21–22).

But he did not proceed to draw the obvious missionary conclusion.

Again, the Israelites acknowledged God as the creator of all; he had called all men, even Israel's worst enemies, into being. Therefore he evidently loved them all. Not a difficult conclusion to draw, but it was only in the closing stages of the Old Testament that it was clearly expressed.

To understand this seemingly illogical situation it is necessary to recall some of the deep tensions that were involved in Israel's paradoxical position as religious unit and political kingdom. A central source of tension was the sharp contrast established between the Chosen People and all the rest of men, the *goyim*, 'the nations'. This contrast appears in a variety of forms in Old Testament literature, in legislation against marriages with foreigners, in prophetic fulminations against Israel's neighbours. It accounts for most of the phrases, especially in the Psalms and the prophetical books, that, in our belatedly ecumenical age, tend to strike a jarring note.

Another element to be taken account of is the Israelites' conviction that they were not merely the Chosen People but that they possessed the Promised Land, which was consequently a chosen country, the home of Yahweh. This thought occurs in strange and striking ways throughout the Old Testament. The stanza from Psalm 137 is familiar—and typical: 'Jerusalem, if I forget you, may my right hand wither!' Israel, and the Jerusalem temple in particular, was the dwelling-place of Yahweh, and those who wished to enter into contact with him had to come to visit him there. Only in his homeland could he be truly worshipped. This is the thought behind the incident described in 2 Kings 5:15–19, where Naaman, a Syrian general cured of his leprosy in Israel, returns to Damascus promising to worship Yahweh there. But, to do so, he brings with him sacks of earth from Israel on which he can stand to pray to the God of Israel in pagan territory. In the early undeveloped stage of Old

Testament thought the Israelites presumed that Yahweh, in becoming their God, had thereby made himself a stranger to the rest of the world. Darkness covered the earth, and the only ray of light from on high fell on the Holy of Holies in the temple. One result of this is that, when universalism is eventually acknowledged, it is seen chiefly as a procession of all mankind to Jerusalem.

> The peoples will stream to it,
> nations without number will come to it; and they will say,
> 'Come, let us go up to the mountain of Yahweh,
> to the Temple of the God of Jacob
> so that he may teach us his ways
> and we may walk in his paths (*Mic.* 4:1–2).

A third constant tension in Old Testament history was Israel's continual struggle for sheer survival as a political and ethnic entity. Israel was a tiny nation surrounded by large and powerful empires; the drama now being played out in the Middle East has had many rehearsals in Old Testament times. The historical books show clearly that Israel could never relax, never extend the hand of friendship confidently to the neighbouring nations, except during that rare moment of harmony in the reign of Solomon. For the rest, the children of Israel were sentinels on the city walls, guardians of the gates and towers, and it is not surprising that the Old Testament should be full of military images and metaphors. Israel was never loved by her neighbours; she was constantly reviled and frequently attacked. She had to struggle to reach the land of promise, then struggle to possess it, and for the rest of her history struggle to hold on to it. In such circumstances it was not humanly possible to go out to the nations in love and generosity and share her riches with them.

This situation had, however, an even deeper consequence, a

final source of religious tension. Since Israel was at the same time a chosen people and a geographical kingdom, her political enemies were automatically her religious enemies also. A small island of monotheism in the great sea of oriental polytheism, Israel's true religion was ever in danger of being swallowed up or stamped out by invasion, or of being insidiously eroded. The bright lights of pagan cities, the temples of foreign gods, the attractions of more lax religions—all beckoned Israel seductively to return to her polytheistic beginnings beyond the Euphrates. Thus the 'high places' of pagan worship within Israel's borders remained a constant temptation all through her history, and were the object of some of the prophets' most scathing attacks.

Thus, as far as Israel's religious destiny was concerned, her neighbours' gods could be as dangerous as their armies. Perhaps the classic example is the good king Solomon; the opening verses of 1 Kings 11 need no comment: 'King Solomon loved many foreign women . . . When Solomon grew old his wives swayed his heart to other gods; and his heart was not wholly with Yahweh his God . . . Solomon became a follower of Astarte, the goddess of the Sidonians, and of Milcom, the Ammonite abomination.'

It is not surprising, then, that the preaching of the prophets so often took the form of stern warnings against the gods of the heathen. Keeping their religion pure from pagan contamination was a full-time occupation for Israel's men of sanctity and wisdom, and this was an effective obstacle to any missionary initiative. The Israelites did not set out deliberately to keep the treasure of their faith from the pagans, but they did feel obliged to keep it safe from pagan influences.

The reason for this, in fact the need for it, becomes clear when we turn the pages of the Old Testament historical books. The story of the Judges, Saul and David knows only one attitude to non-Israelites—fight against them, destroy them if possible, as potentially dangerous enemies. In all her history Israel experienced no friendship, no outstretched helping hand; hers was a lonely struggle for survival—a continuation on a different level of her earlier struggle as a nomadic tribe in the hostile desert sands. Abraham strove for the survival of the clan; Moses legislated for the survival of the people; the kings waged war for the survival of the nation. Israel had to resign herself to being regarded as an intruder, unwanted and unwelcomed, an obvious target to be raided for slaves and flocks. She was never considered as having anything to give, as having a message of hope and destiny for the lives of those who gazed grimly and rapaciously across her borders. In brief, Israel's consciousness of her uniqueness as the one chosen race of Yahweh, and her incessant struggle for survival, combined to form a kind of siege mentality and an inward-looking, Jerusalem-centred religion that could not succeed in blossoming into a missionary mentality.

So it became necessary for God to give Israel many reminders, in word and deed, of her true destiny vis-à-vis the whole of humanity. It was not always easy to communicate the message that the God who had chosen Israel to be his own also wished ultimately to draw all races and men within the arms of his love. But the fact is written clearly enough in the Old Testament story.

It emerges, first of all, from the Israelites' understanding of the pre-Abraham commerce between God and men. The biblical story of the origins and early days of humanity is studded with unmistakable statements of universality—God's love for all men, and his plans to translate that love into action. It is interesting that the darkest moments in those early gropings of mankind are redeemed by promises of a universal salvation. For example, right after the primeval tragedy of the Fall comes the promise of humanity's victory over the serpent Satan: 'I will make you enemies of each other: you and the

woman, your offspring and her offspring. It will crush your
head and you will strike its heel' (*Gen.* 3:15). No matter which
interpretation of this difficult text we accept, it is clear that all
humanity is, in some way or other, involved in the ultimate
triumph over Satan. No limitations of race or creed can be
read into this text.

Similarly, immediately after the punishment of the Flood
comes an unexpected expression of divine affection—the
covenant with Noah recorded in Genesis 9. 'Here is the sign
of the Covenant I make between myself and you and every
living creature with you for all generations. I set my bow in the
clouds and it shall be a sign of the Covenant between me and
the earth. When I gather the clouds over the earth and the bow
appears in the clouds, I will recall the Covenant between myself
and you and every living creature of every kind. . . . When
the bow is in the clouds I shall see it and call to mind the
lasting Covenant between God and every living creature of
every kind that is found on the earth' (*Gen.* 9:12–16). Notice
the almost monotonous repetition of the universalist theme in
these verses, and in the surrounding ones: 'every living
creature for all generations'. It is highly significant that the first
mention of covenant in the Bible should occur in such a
universalist context, long before any covenant made with the
Patriarchs or with Israel as a people. Surely the essential
message of this is that the original and enduring divine plan is
concerned with the salvation of all men—and this plan was
neither altered nor annulled by the later specific covenants with
individuals or with the group. Genesis 9 is stated in the widest
possible terms and is unconnected with details of religious
observance. And therefore the sign is as universal as the
covenant—'my bow in the clouds', the rainbow, capable of
being seen and understood by all men everywhere as a reminder
of the God who made and loves them all.

The brighter side to the Old Testament attitude towards 'the rest of men' emerges also from a closer reading of the apparently 'anti-*goyim*' texts and from a consideration of their historical and literary contexts. It is quite untrue to say that the Old Testament regarded all non-Israelites as a desolate *massa damnata*. Let's look at the facts.

The harshest words against the *goyim* are contained in the prophetic passages that take the literary form of 'judgements against the nations', for example, Amos 1–2; Jeremiah 46–51. But these are judgements passed, not on the religious deficiencies or limitations or ignorance of the peoples concerned, but on their crimes against their fellows—the cruelty, the oppression of the poor, the haughtiness, the egoism, the unconcealed joy in lording it over their brothers. They are not condemned for their failure to share Israel's respect for her God, but for their failure to show respect for their fellow-men.

Israelite legislation, except for the war-time ethic of *herem* (which demanded total destruction of an enemy), was careful to provide for the humane treatment of *goyim*, 'the strangers' living within her boundaries. 'If a stranger lives with you in your land, do not molest him. You must count him as one of your own countrymen and love him as yourself—for you were once strangers yourselves in Egypt. I am Yahweh your God' (*Lev.* 19:33–34). 'It is he (Yahweh) who sees justice done for the orphan and the widow, who loves the stranger and gives him food and clothing. Love the stranger then, for you were strangers in the land of Egypt' (*Deut.* 10:18–19). 'The strangers' were creatures of the great Yahweh and carried, even if unconsciously, that faint spark of the divine that sets the human on a plane apart from all other created things.

The unity of all mankind, in origin and in terminus, is never once cast in doubt by the Old Testament. God's choice of Israel was a free divine decision, not based on human merit or exclusiveness. In spite of all the erroneous conclusions that Israel occasionally drew from her selection—the national pride and religious snobbery—the fact that all men and all nations formed one family was never entirely forgotten. For instance after the return from the Babylonian captivity, while the laws against marriage with the *goyim* were being renewed with harsh vigour, the Jerusalem priestly school underscored the unity of all mankind by the Genesis genealogies (chs. 5, 10, 11). And the Tower of Babel narrative (*Gen.* 11:1–9) presupposes an original unity of culture as well as of nature. Against much forced and false exegesis prompted by particular prejudices, it must be maintained that the Old Testament gives no basis for theories of racial superiority. Amos saw this clearly and expressed it in his usual abrupt fashion:

> Are not you and the Cushites all the same to me,
> sons of Israel?—it is Yahweh who speaks.
> Did not I, who brought Israel out of the land of Egypt,
> bring the Philistines from Caphtor, and the Aramaeans
> from Kir? (*Amos* 9:7).

By far the most significant aspect of Israel's attitude to her pagan neighbours is the conviction, repeated so often and so explicitly in the Old Testament, that pagan characters could act both as valid messengers for God and as striking examples of pious living. And this is more than merely mentioned in the text; both the words used and the contexts chosen seem deliberately arranged to underline the fact. It is enough to indicate a few:

Melchizedek—a mysterious figure, pagan priest-king of Salem, who blessed Abraham, and who lived on in Israelite thought as an ideal of priesthood (*Gen.* 14:18–20).

Balaam—a pagan seer of Moab, who is used by Yahweh to sing the praises of Israel before a hostile king (*Num.* 22–24).

Ruth—a Moabite girl presented as a model of filial devotion and true charity to her widowed mother-in-law (*Ruth* 1).

Job—from the land of Uz, in Edom, an area held in particular contempt by Israel, one who is described as 'a sound and honest man who feared God and shunned evil' (*Job* 1).

Although Israel's destiny as a mediating people was never put into effective execution, it was understood perfectly by the literary redactors of Israel's history. And we find it mentioned expressly right at the very point where Israel's exclusiveness begins—the call of Abraham. 'Leave your country, your family and your father's house, for the land I will show you. I will make you a great nation; I will bless you and make your name so famous that it will be used as a blessing. I will bless those who bless you: I will curse those who slight you. All the tribes of the earth will bless themselves by you' (*Gen.* 12:1-3). This is not, then, a prize to a favourite child, but a gift and a message to 'all the tribes of the earth'.

The call of Abraham is a missionary vocation, not because he was led out from his own country and hearth, but because he was called for the benefit of others, and in this case for the benefit of the whole family of man. His posterity will turn out to be a universal Church, a meaning that the Israelites could not have grasped from Genesis 15:5: 'Look up to heaven and count the stars if you can. Such will be your descendants.' Nor could Abraham have fully understood the true significance of his call, or its pivotal place in the whole range of salvation history. Looking back across the pages of the Bible story from our vantage point in the days of fulfilment we can see, a little more clearly, the outlines of the divine plan. The salvation story, as recorded in the Bible, from the call of Abraham to the Acts of the Apostles, is simply a chain of events linking together two great masses of paganism chronologically separated by almost 2,000 years. Out of the vast mysterious paganism of the Orient in the nineteenth century B.C., Abraham was called by God. And from Abraham the salvation story flows in a direct line of physical descent to Christ and the apostles. Christ sent his apostles out into the new paganism of the Roman empire—the final step in the long journey on which Abraham had set out. Abraham was called out of paganism in order that the apostles might one day be sent back into paganism, to bring to unbelievers the fruits of everything that had happened in the meantime. This is what makes St Paul gasp in wonder: 'It was God's purpose to reveal it to them and to show all the rich glory of this mystery to pagans' (*Col.* 1:27). Thus, in calling Abraham, God neither abandoned nor rejected the rest of mankind; instead he prepared the way for their ultimate salvation.

The pattern evident in the vocation of Abraham is repeated in the series of calls and covenants granted by God to succeeding Patriarchs. It is sufficient to read Genesis 28:10–22—the incident of Jacob's dream. 'Your descendants shall be like the specks of dust on the ground; you shall spread to the west and the east, to the north and the south, and all the tribes of the earth shall bless themselves by you and your descendants' (v. 14).

Abraham and his descendants wandered over the whole Near East, wondered about the plans and methods of their new-found God, fought, worried, and succeeded in preserving the clan. Neither famine in Canaan nor tyranny in Egypt could defeat the spirit that sprang from the original promise: 'I will make your descendants like the dust on the ground' (*Gen.* 13:16).

Then Moses came on the scene—messenger of Yahweh and liberator of the people destined to be Yahweh's own. Again, it is worth pausing here to see the missionary nature of Moses' task. God sent him back from Jethro and the desert to his countrymen in Egypt, not merely to lead them out from slavery to precarious freedom, not merely to lead them from a hostile despot to a land of their own, but chiefly to lead them to know and worship the one true God. Also, Moses achieved this by mediating at Mount Sinai—the finest hour in all salvation history—the sealing of the covenant between God and his people. This was a covenant in the true biblical meaning of the word, not a hard bargain driven between God and men, not a cold legal exchange of obligations. It was rather a pledge of loyalty: God pledging himself to be faithful to his chosen children, Israel pledging herself to be faithful in the exclusive worship and service of her God. This was a human response of gratitude and trust to a God who had worked deliverance and who would do far greater things in the future. Any missionary who has led a group of catechumens to a know-ledge of the incarnation and redemption and joined them to Christ in the waters of baptism can readily appreciate the missionary nature of the career of Moses.

However, to find the missionary ideals of Israel we must turn to her preaching and prayer—to the prophetical books and the Psalms. And in scanning the prophetic and wisdom literature of the Old Testament we can distinguish four stages in Israel's approach to a genuinely missionary mentality. These are not neat, water-tight divisions; they are an attempt to show approximately the steps by which Israelite thinking moved forward. They do not always follow the chronological order of writing, for two reasons: first, some giant figures, like the anonymous author of Deutero-Isaiah, leaped far into the unknown ahead of their fellows; second, we are not always able to establish with certainty the date at which a passage first went into circulation in Israelite religious circles. It is always fascinating and instructive to watch somebody increase in knowledge and understanding, and this is just as true of a group as of an individual. One of the most rewarding aspects of Old Testament study is the tracing of the thought of Israel as it progresses from the first vague intimations of the Patriarchs to the more profound and luminous understanding of the last wisdom writers.

We know that biblical prophecy suffered from severe

limitations in details of time and method. The prophets were God's spokesmen, but their vision of the future, which was, after all, a purely incidental element in their preaching, was mainly in general terms and in pretty blurred images. It was, however, founded on genuine illumination, not on wild dreams, and as they strained, with extreme difficulty, to comprehend God's designs for the future, they did see the dawn of a brighter era—one of universal submission to Yahweh. It is obviously impossible, in the space of a few pages, to do justice to the volume and variety of the prophetic witness on the subject of universalism, but we can indicate some sample passages.

1. As Israel grew in appreciation and understanding of her own election, of her knowledge of the one true God and the intimacy with him to which she had been admitted, she sensed that spectators of her privileged position would eventually wish to come and share it. The surrounding peoples would surely arrive one day at the gates of the temple, begging for admission to saving contact with the God of Israel.

> All the pagans will come and adore you, Lord,
> all will glorify your name,
> since you alone are great, you perform marvels,
> you God, you alone (*Ps.* 86:9–10).

Jeremiah looks forward to the messianic era in similar terms: 'When that time comes, Jerusalem shall be called: The Throne of Yahweh; all the nations will gather there in the name of Yahweh and will no longer follow the dictates of their own stubborn hearts' (3:17). This was evidently a preaching theme popular before the exile, as it is found, in almost identical words, in Isaiah 2:1–4 and Micah 4:1–4. But this much we must notice: there is no indication here that Israel feels called to take an active role in leading the nations to Jerusalem.

Rather, the prophets present an optimistic picture of a future in which, somehow, with no effort on Israel's part, the nations will finally acknowledge the superiority of Yahweh and come in procession to his holy city.

2. A less temple-centred vision occurs in several Psalms, particularly the Psalms of kingship; as an example, this is Psalm 47:8–9:

> God is king of the nations,
> he reigns on his holy throne.
> The leaders of the nations rally
> to the people of the God of Abraham.
> Every shield in the world belongs to God.
> He reigns supreme.

But there is little advance in thought; the liturgical image of the temple has been replaced by the military image of a victorious king over the nations. It is a martial and triumphalistic vision of the Messiah, and again, Israel's role is purely passive—to wait for the happy day when all men will fall down and accept the yoke of Yahweh.

3. A considerable step forward is made as Israel becomes aware of her duty to be a public witness to the goodness and kindness of her God—to sing the praises of Yahweh in the view and hearing of all men. This idea is never developed in detail, but is mentioned in passing in many Psalms.

> For this I will praise you, Yahweh, among the heathen
> and sing praise to your name (Ps. 18:49).

> Lord, I mean to thank you among the peoples,
> to play music to you among the nations;
> your love is high as heaven,
> your faithfulness as the clouds (Ps. 57:9–10).

In spite of the fleeting nature of the references, there is real progress here: Israel realises that she must be active in proposing her God to the gentiles; it is not enough to sit down and wait for them to arrive at the temple gates. But the concept of going forth to the nations to spread good news is still sadly absent.

4. The fifty-year period of the Babylonian captivity in the sixth century B.C. was dominated by two great prophetic figures, Deutero-Isaiah and Ezekiel. Of the two, Deutero-Isaiah is the intellectual leader. He takes a giant stride forward towards a true understanding of Israel's role in the world, her obligations to her less privileged neighbours and the means by which God will accomplish his plan for a universal salvation. Deutero-Isaiah's inspired thinking on these subjects finds expression chiefly in the famous Servant Songs, in which his thought soars to an apex of piercing clarity and magnificent poetry. Let some snatches of the text speak for themselves.

> I, Yahweh, have called you to serve the cause of right;
> I have taken you by the hand and formed you;
> I have appointed you as covenant of the people and light
> of the nations,
> to open the eyes of the blind,
> to free captives from prison,
> and those who live in darkness from the dungeon.
> My name is Yahweh,
> I will not yield my glory to another,
> nor my honour to idols (42:6–8).

> It is not enough for you to be my servant,
> to restore the tribes of Jacob and bring back the survivors
> of Israel;
> I will make you the light of the nations
> so that my salvation may reach to the ends of the earth (49:6).

Here we find the germ of some ideas that are refreshingly

new in Israelite thought. First, there will be a going forth to the nations, either by an individual or a group. The former passive attitude has given way to an active one—to go out and carry a message to men, to bring light to those in darkness. Besides, the servant will go out not to dominate but to serve. His weapons will not be terror and trumpet blasts, but gentleness and compassion. This is a profoundly different and more dynamic vision of Israel's ancient privilege—that she should be the minister of her good fortune to her neighbours.

But there is a greater and nobler vision to come, in the fourth and final Servant Song, Isaiah 52:13—53:12. This is the servant who suffers, appallingly and innocently, and people turn away their faces from him. But they do not know that

> . . . ours were the sufferings he bore,
> ours the sorrows he carried.
> But we, we thought of him as someone punished,
> struck by God and brought low.
> Yet he was pierced through for our faults,
> crushed for our sins.
> On him lies a punishment that brings us peace,
> and through his wounds we are healed (53:4–5).

This is a new and startling idea in Old Testament theology—that the suffering of one can heal the ills of many. It is at this point that Deutero-Isaiah crosses the threshold into the New Testament, because the picture of the Servant given here could not be drawn from Israel herself, but only from some future servant of Yahweh who would suffer, not for his own sins but for those of others. Thus, in this final song, Deutero-Isaiah paints a frighteningly realistic picture of the tortured body, the heart-broken mother and the darkened skies of Calvary nearly 600 years later. And in so doing he foretells a necessary dimension of all missionary activity, because suffering, patiently borne, is still a price that must be paid, and a means that can be used, for the extension of God's gentle reign over hearts.

With this vision of God's victory over men through service and suffering, the Old Testament reaches its high-water mark of missionary idealism. In the post-exilic period that followed, there was much confusion, and the high heroic call of Deutero-Isaiah seems to have faded away. The renewed legislation against marriage to non-Jews, the Maccabees' brave stand against an impious king, the narrow legalism of the Pharisees—these produced a climate in which the prophetic missionary ideas could not easily be carried over into action. But though practical realisation was delayed, the prophetic voices were not stilled. It is, in fact, in this final period that we come upon two of the most missionary-minded statements of all the Old Testament—in Trito-Isaiah and Jonah.

Some time after the return from the exile, an unknown disciple of the great Deutero-Isaiah added some of his own reflections to his master's voice; they form the third part of our present book of Isaiah, chapters 56–66. Pushing his teacher's thesis to its logical conclusion, he foresees a real missionary exodus to the 'nations', and a day when the nations themselves will chant the wonders of Yahweh.

> I am coming to gather the nations of every language. They shall come to witness my glory. I will give them a sign and send some of their survivors to the nations: to Tarshish, Put, Lud, Moshech, Rosh, Tubal, and Javan, to the distant islands that have never heard of me or seen my glory. They will proclaim my glory to the nations. . . .
> And of some of them I will make priests and Levites, says Yahweh. . . .
> From New Moon to New Moon,
> from sabbath to sabbath,
> all mankind will come to bow down
> in my presence, says Yahweh (*Is.* 66:18–23).

Unexpectedly, the deceptively simple book of Jonah provides the clearest picture of Israel's missionary obligation and the most damning denunciation of her narrow nationalist outlook. Wrapping his message in popular story form, the author presents God as ordering a Jewish prophet to preach repentance to the Assyrians. The Assyrians were probably the most detested of all Judah's enemies, and no Jew could have much enthusiasm for a missionary expedition to them. In spite of his schemes to go elsewhere, the prophet finds himself in Nineveh, and so has to convey his message of warning. To his obvious disgust, the Assyrians listen and repent. Sulking in the shade of a plant temporarily provided by Yahweh, the prophet laments his fate and concludes: 'I might as well be dead as go on living.' His combination of self-righteousness and self-pity earns God's rebuke in the closing verses of the book: 'You are only upset about a castor-oil plant which cost you no labour, which you did not make grow, which sprouted in a night and has perished in a night. And am I not to feel sorry for Nineveh, the great city, in which there are more than a hundred and twenty thousand people who cannot tell their right hand from their left, to say nothing of all the animals?' (*Jon.* 4:10–11). Thus, the whole point of the Jonah story is that God is ready to love, pity and pardon all men, even cruel tyrants like the Assyrians. This was a hard lesson for people accustomed to consider themselves as the apple of Yahweh's eye, but it is the clearest voice of Old Testament times proclaiming God as universal Father, who wills all his creatures to be saved. In this sense, it is a fitting end to the Old Testament missionary story.

Perhaps now we are in a position to understand the two sides of Israel's attitude to pagans, to the spiritually dispossessed. We must accept the fact that there was, in the Old Testament, no missionary activity worth mentioning. Much has been written about Christ's accusation against the Pharisees: 'Alas for you, scribes and Pharisees, you hypocrites! You who travel over sea and land to make a single proselyte, and when you have him you make him twice as fit for hell as you are' (*Matt.* 23:15). Commentators dispute the real meaning of the phrase, but most agree that even in the period of the Diaspora there was no organised effort at conversion. Theoretically, the Diaspora provided an ideal launching-pad for missionary endeavour, but it was put to effective use only by Paul, and then for the spread of Christianity, not Judaism. The fact remains that the Old Testament contains neither a compelling motive nor an explicit command to share Israel's faith with the world. As we shall see, Christ brought both the motive and the command.

Even though Judaism was not a missionary religion, at the same time it must be said that the Old Testament is a missionary book. Israel's thinkers and theologians had come to see that salvation was not to the Jews only, but through the Jews to all humanity. But only Jeremiah and the Isaian school seem to have grasped the truth that some great divine intervention in history must first take place before the pious wishes of Israel will be translated into an active apostolate. This is the central message of Jeremiah's splendid 'new covenant' prophecy in chapter 31.

> See, the days are coming—it is Yahweh who speaks— when I will make a new covenant with the House of Israel (and the House of Judah), but not a covenant like the one I made with their ancestors on the day I took them by the hand to bring them out of the land of Egypt. They broke that covenant of mine, so I had to show them who was master. It is Yahweh who speaks. No, this is the covenant I will make with the House of Israel when those days arrive—it is Yahweh who speaks. Deep within them I will plant my Law, writing it on their hearts. Then I will be their God and they shall be my people. There will be

no further need for neighbour to try to teach neighbour, or brother to say to brother, 'Learn to know Yahweh!' No, they will all know me, the least no less than the greatest—it is Yahweh who speaks—since I will forgive their iniquity and never call their sin to mind (*Jer.* 31: 31–34).

This new law of God, written in men's hearts, can only be the result of a special intervention of Yahweh, because it will take the form of an internal personal renewal that can have no author but God. It will be based on a knowledge of God and of his plans for men that only God himself could give. What Jeremiah could not have foreseen was that this new salvific act of God would also be the final act of Judaism, accomplished by the unique Servant of Yahweh who was God-made-Jew— Jesus of Nazareth.

5 The New Testament—A Missionary Mandate

Since Jesus was the long-awaited Messiah of Jewish hopes, it is only natural that the early sections of the New Testament should introduce him in Old Testament terms. We find the familiar prophetic images of the messianic mission colouring the whole Infancy account in Matthew and Luke. The wise men of the gentiles came to Jerusalem in search of him (*Matt.* 2); Joseph is told that Mary's son will 'save his people from their sins' (*Matt.* 1); Simeon spoke of him as 'a light to enlighten the pagans' (*Luke* 2). In these opening chapters there is no advance on the traditional Old Testament position; it is not yet clear that God's salvation plan involves opening 'the door of faith to the pagans' (*Acts* 14) by going out to proclaim the Good News to them rather than by waiting for God to call them to the temple.

What makes the New Testament 'new' is its central act, the redemption, and because of that act everything will change. This is an act of divine love so extraordinary, so stunning in its magnitude, that nothing could really have prepared men for it. And the results are as prodigal as the act—infinite good news for every man coming into the world. Since the Son of God did not remain at his Father's right hand in heaven but came into the world as the Son of Man to accomplish redemption, so the good news of his redemption will not remain sealed in some sheltered and elusive Treasure Island. Christ, through his Church, will send out messengers, generation after generation, to carry this news to the furthest corners of the earth and the most remote bush villages. Thus, only by incarnation and redemption was the true dynamism of divine love unleashed.

In order to trace the development of the missionary idea in the New Testament, let us examine the evidence in three stages:

    i) Christ's public ministry—synoptic gospels,
    ii) the post-Resurrection period—Matthew 28,
    iii) the expanding Church—Paul and John.

(i) *The Public Ministry*

The first impression gained from turning the pages of the synoptic gospels is one of unrestrained universality: the kingdom of God is at hand, and it will affect the lives of all men everywhere and to the end of time. In preparing the minds of his audience for the Messiah about to appear on the river bank, John the Baptist had warned the Jews against trusting too much in their genealogy: '. . . do not presume to tell yourselves, "We have Abraham for our father", because, I tell you, God can raise children for Abraham from these stones' (*Matt.* 3:9). The phrases from Christ's sermons and parables are too numerous to mention, and are happily familiar. He addresses his disciples as the light of the world, not of Israel, and as the salt of the earth, not of Palestine. The universalist tone of the parables is unmistakable: 'the field is the world'; 'it grew and became a tree, and the birds of the air sheltered in its branches'.

However, there are some difficulties that must be faced squarely. First of all, Christ's witness to his Father seems to have been limited to his fellow-Jews; he did visit non-Jewish territories briefly, but there is no evidence that he preached there. Also, some phrases attributed to Christ in the synoptic gospels reflect unfavourably on the gentiles, for example: 'In your prayers do not babble as the pagans do, for they think that by using many words they will make themselves heard'

(*Matt.* 6:7). Some of his instructions to the Twelve prior to their preliminary mission have a disturbing sound: 'Do not turn your steps to pagan territory, and do not enter any Samaritan town; go rather to the lost sheep of the House of Israel' (*Matt.* 10:5–6). And many readers have been scandalised by his abrupt reply to the despairing Canaanite woman: 'I was sent only to the lost sheep of the House of Israel. . . . It is not fair to take the children's food and throw it to the house-dogs' (*Matt.* 15:24, 26).

Two facts about these texts strike one immediately: they all occur in Matthew, and all in the first section of his gospel. These facts are instructive. Matthew's gospel was written by a Jew, and chiefly for Jewish readers, and therefore it contains many nuances that are of specifically Jewish origin and for obviously Jewish consumption. Here, as always, Christ's message is expressed, not in *ipsissima verba,* but through a human mouthpiece. Again, it is now unanimously accepted by New Testament scholars that the 'Galilean crisis' of chapters 16–17 of Matthew—Peter's profession of faith and the transfiguration—marks a real turning-point in Christ's public life and in the orientation of his ministry. The idyllic early days of Galilee were over; now Christ set his face towards Jerusalem and the cross. In doing so he turned his back definitively on the synagogue and announced, with increasing clarity, his universal mission. This is made brutally clear to the Jews in Matthew 21:43: 'I tell you, then, that the kingdom of God will be taken from you and given to a people who will produce its fruit'. Not surprisingly, from this moment onward the hostility of the Jewish leaders to Christ mounted in fury; they determined to hound him to death—and did so.

It may be worth looking a little more closely at these apparently troublesome texts.

Matthew 6:7: It is interesting to notice that Luke, in the corresponding passage (ch. 6), omits all reference to pagans, and renders a similar phrase in Matthew 5:47 ('Even the pagans do as much, do they not?') harmless by substituting 'sinners' for 'pagans'. To be honest, an unprejudiced gentile could hardly take offence at Matthew's phrase; it is a statement of fact, not of contempt. The Jews prided themselves on their superiority to the gentiles in matters religious; and, after all, they did have the advantage of the Law and the prophets.

Matthew 10:5–6: Again it is intriguing to see that both Mark and Luke, in recording the mission of the Twelve, omit these 'offensive' verses. They were writing for a more cosmopolitan public than Matthew. But we still have to answer the question: why this apparently unreasonable and racial prohibition? Some commentators take the line of least resistance here and reply that it reflects a redaction by a Judaising group in the early Christian community. While not impossible, this explanation has little to recommend it. It is more reasonable, and more scientific, to take account of the context and note that this incident takes place early in the disciples' training period, and thus it is by no means strange that their mission should be limited to less difficult and hostile circumstances. Also, as we shall see, Christ was always keenly aware that the Jews had been chosen by his Father to receive the Old Law, and he felt it fitting that they should be the first to be offered the New Law.

Matthew 15:24: Here it is illuminating to put the accounts of Matthew and Mark side by side.

Matt. 15	Mark 7
I was sent only to the lost sheep of the House of Israel.	—— ——
It is not fair to take the children's food and throw it to the house-dogs.	The children should be fed first, because it is not fair to take the children's food and throw it to the house-dogs.

Mark's phrase seems designed to explain Christ's approach during the early part of his ministry—the word 'first' provides the key. The Jews were his first care, but not his only one. He did not claim that the pagans would never 'be fed', but that they would not be fed 'first'. And this was the order of priority later followed by Paul, as the Acts of the Apostles shows: 'We had to proclaim the word of God to you first, but since you have rejected it, since you do not think yourselves worthy of eternal life, we must turn to the pagans' (*Acts* 13 :46). Luke 24:47 echoes the same thought: '. . . to all the nations, beginning from Jerusalem'.

Besides, such phrases do not limit in any way the universality of the messianic mission, even in this first part of Christ's preaching career. After all, he did grant the request of the gentile woman, adding: 'Woman, you have great faith.' He did heal the pitiful creatures in Transjordan, even though the gentile population there responded by imploring 'him to leave the neighbourhood' (*Matt.* 8:34). Even his choice of the title 'Son of Man' is significant. Its source is the book of Daniel, and this is part of Daniel's vision of the Son of Man:

> On him was conferred sovereignty,
> glory and kingship,
> and men of all peoples, nations and languages became his
> servants. (*Dan.* 7:14).

While Christ did not address his message specifically to the gentiles at any point, his whole approach and method provide the blueprint for missionary activity and mentality. He showed his disciples, by deed more than by word, that the Old Testament attitude of passive waiting for the kingdom of God was not the means of conversion decided upon by his Father. The kingdom is finally here; he inaugurates it, but his followers must carry it to men. Christ did not sit at the temple gates, as

Jeremiah had done, and wait for men to come and hear his message. He did not remain by the river Jordan, as John the Baptist had done. Instead, he travelled the length and breadth of Palestine, to big towns and little towns; he carried the kingdom to the doorsteps of every household in Galilee and Judæa. 'Jesus made a tour through all the towns and villages, teaching in their synagogues, proclaiming the Good News of the kingdom and curing all kinds of diseases and sickness' (*Matt.* 9:35). There, in a word, is Christ's missionary programme—going from village to village, bringing the word of deliverance and practical acts of charity to support it. It is still our apostolic programme.

Luke marks the opening of the second section of Christ's public ministry with the phrase: 'Now as the time drew near for him to be taken up to heaven, he resolutely took the road for Jerusalem' (9:51). Geographically he was moving towards Jerusalem and death, but historically he was moving away from Jerusalem and her ancient privileges towards his universal mission. In this second section the Jews, misled by their spiritual chiefs, hardened their attitude against Christ, and he directed his apostles' vision more and more to wider harvests. Thus it is in this section of the narrative that Luke has placed the most striking universalist statements. The concept of the salvation of the gentiles is expressed with increasing clarity: the Good Samaritan, the lost sheep ('go after the missing one'). No one is excluded from the fruits of his passion; for example, the institution of the Eucharist—'. . . the blood of the covenant, which is to be poured out for many'.

With this phrase, anticipating his death and resurrection, Christ inaugurates the new economy of salvation, seals the new covenant and offers redemption to 'many', that is to the multitude. The word is an obvious allusion to the Suffering Servant:

By his sufferings shall my servant justify many,
taking their faults on himself (*Is.* 53:11).

Thus the 'many' means the nations, the gentiles—and so has a
direct and unlimited missionary significance. This had already
been stated unequivocally in Matthew's eschatological discourse: 'This Good News of the kingdom will be proclaimed
to the whole world as a witness to all the nations. And then
the end will come' (24:14).

We still have not answered the question: why did Christ not
personally engage in a missionary approach to the nations?
Why was his teaching and preaching career restricted to the
Jews? On the basis of the New Testament evidence the reasons
would seem to be two. First, Christ revealed the universality
of the kingdom of God only gradually. This is perfectly in
harmony with other aspects of his ministry; the unveiling of
his messiahship and, even more so, of his divinity, was done
slowly. He did not abruptly snatch Israel's ancient privileges
from her hands; he offered the Jews the opportunity of being
the first to embrace the new covenant. Only when their lack
of comprehension was clearly established did he pronounce the
inevitable result: 'Then there will be weeping and grinding of
teeth, when you see Abraham and Isaac and Jacob and all the
prophets in the kingdom of God, and yourselves turned outside.
And men from east and west, from north and south, will come
to take their places at the feast in the kingdom of God' (*Luke*
13:28–29). This must not be interpreted as a condemnation of
Israel, but rather as a factual description of a situation—the
situation over which St Paul agonised so painfully in Romans
9–11.

However, in the theology of the salvation plan there is a more
profound reason for Christ's restriction of his personal mission,
and that of his apostles during his lifetime, to the Jews. A
universal mission has neither meaning nor motive until two

conditions are met: that the one sent has something of value to bring; that he has the necessary aid to deliver his message. Before Christ can send out his followers on their mission to the ends of the earth, salvation must first be accomplished, and the Spirit must have come. Christ's death is the open door through which all men can return to their Father; there is no ambiguity in John's phrase: 'And when I am lifted up from the earth, I shall draw all men to myself' (12:32). Christ could, of course, have anticipated all this in his personal mission, but he chose to leave to his followers the honour of putting universalism into action. But only after his death and resurrection have they the historical Good News to carry, and only after the coming of the Spirit have they the light and the courage necessary to carry it without fear or favour. He obliges them to stay in Jerusalem until the Spirit come: 'Stay in the city then, until you are clothed with the power from on high' (*Luke* 24:49). In short, the missionary message of the Bible passes from the ideal to the real order only after, and by means of, Christ's passion and Pentecost. Thus it is to the final section of the gospels and the opening section of the Acts of the Apostles that we must turn to find the genuine expression of the New Testament missionary dynamism.

ii) *The post-Resurrection Period*

The missionary mandate to the Church, recorded by all three synoptists, occurs naturally, then, in the post-resurrection section of the gospels. This does not necessarily mean that the command was given by Christ at this particular time, or in any of the precise formulae found in the gospels; it does mean that the evangelists, in assembling and ordering the material they drew from the primitive catechesis, saw that the missionary mandate can be properly understood only in connection with this period of expectation between Easter and Pentecost. This period links the three historical events on which missionary impetus depends: Christ's passion, his glorification by resurrection and ascension, and the continuation of his work through men by the power of his Spirit.

When we recall the facility with which the synoptists introduce discrepancies of detail and wording into their accounts, there is a remarkable similarity between the five texts which relay the missionary command. This shows that it was a familiar item in the basic catechesis of the young Christian community.

	Content	*Destination*
Matt. 24:14	This Good News of the kingdom as a witness	to the whole world to all the nations
Matt. 28:18	Go, therefore, make disciples	of all the nations
Mark 16:15	Proclaim the Good News	to all creation Go out to the whole world
Luke 24:47	Repentance for the forgiveness of sins	to all the nations, beginning from Jerusalem
Acts 1:8	You will be my witnesses	not only in Jerusalem but throughout Judaea and Samaria, and indeed to the ends of the earth.

It is easy to see that these texts present three essential elements of the missionary apostolate: a) an active going forth: go;

proclaim; preach; witness. *b*) a message of hope: Good News; forgiveness of sins. *c*) an unlimited horizon: the whole world; all the nations; all creation; the ends of the earth. It is in the light of these three elements that we must yet, even today, evaluate any missionary theory or achievement.

It has been pointed out that, in the post-resurrection narratives, there are two types of incident described. One deals with Christ and the good women who wept over him, and these events underline chiefly the fact that he is risen and that the risen Lord is genuinely the crucified Christ. For example, 'There is no need for you to be afraid. I know you are looking for Jesus, who was crucified. He is not here, for he has risen, as he said he would' (*Matt.* 28:5–6). The second type consists of encounters between the risen Christ and the apostles, and here the theme is always that of giving witness to all men of what they have seen and heard—the life, death and triumphant rising of their Lord. Thus, the contacts recounted between Christ and the apostles in this period are set precisely in the context of missions. And always the mission is a universal one.

Now, let us turn to look, in more detail, at one of these incidents, the one described in Matthew 28:16–20, the final verses of Matthew's gospel, and the most explicit and best-known version of the missionary mandate.

> All authority in heaven and on earth has been given to me. Go, therefore, make disciples of all the nations; baptise them in the name of the Father and of the Son and of the Holy Spirit, and teach them to observe all the commands I gave you. And know that I am with you always; yes, to the end of time (vv. 18–20).

In terms of our present knowledge of the process by which the gospels were formed, it is possible to say that these words represent a catechetical formula of the primitive Church, and that the Trinitarian expression of baptism is a trace of an early liturgical text. But while the formula is that of the early Christians, the thought, the meaning and the message are directly those of Christ. As Matthew transmits it, there are three clearly defined units of thought in the text: a statement; a command; a promise. We can pause for some comments on each, taken mainly from the lecture of Fr J. Schutte, S.V.D.

Statement: 'All authority in heaven and on earth has been given to me.' This is the theological fact on which the whole mandate is based—Christ's universal sovereignty as Lord of all. It is important to notice the connection made between this and the following verse, the command itself: 'All authority . . . has been given to me. Go, *therefore,* make disciples . . .'. In other words, Christ *sends* because he has authority to send; he sends *us* because he has power to send us; he sends us to the *nations* because he has authority over the nations. Christ claims a total, utterly unrestricted lordship; this is expressed in each of the three parts of the text: *all* authority; *all* the nations; *all* the commands; *always.*

It is by virtue of this unlimited lordship of Christ over men and ages that we are missionaries, and, as missionaries, we go forth armed with Christ's supreme authority, no matter where, when or to whom we go. No rights, either of natural law or of civil power, are exempt from his universal lordship. Thus, in preaching the Good News of Christ's salvation and redemption, we never invade a foreign territory; rather, like the Israelites of old, we take possession of a promised land. Every time we lead people to Christ's knowledge and love, this simply means that Christ takes formal possession of what belongs to him by right, because given to him by his Father.

Command: 'Go, therefore, make disciples of all the nations; baptise them in the name of the Father and of the Son and of the Holy Spirit, and teach them to observe all the commands I gave you.' The essential phrase here is the opening one, the command proper; the other two clauses merely bring greater precision by indicating the basic elements involved in 'making disciples'. And they turn out to be the two normal methods of catechesis—word and sacrament. But they depend on the first word 'Go'. This imperative verb marks the end of the Old Testament concept of a witnessing people. The Israelites always concluded that they should witness to God by remaining within their borders and waiting for men to come, as to a shrine. On us the duty lies of taking the initiative, of going forth to find men. In the Christian vocabulary, 'evangelisation' means 'exile'.

Our task is to 'make disciples'. It is not enough to proclaim the message; we must use every talent and strain every effort to persuade men to become disciples, that is, men willing to follow, to love and to imitate Christ. To be a disciple has nothing in common with an 'anonymous' or vague attachment; it is to be a committed and convinced believer. This is what a missionary aims at, and he can stop at nothing less. Much is being said and written now about the 'presence' of the Church, as if mere presence were the final aim of missions. Perhaps this is a consolation for the faint-hearted, but it is not enough for the true missionary. The Church is not merely Christ present but Christ active in today's world. We can never be satisfied to say that the Church is present in a mission territory; the Church must be active there, ministering the charity of her Founder to all comers, the grateful and the ungrateful, the wise and the not-so-wise. A local church content to be a discreet and polite presence, careful to avoid conflict with a political power, right or wrong, can lead to—and historically has several times led to—a warped and distorted image of Christ. The Church must courageously continue to bring men face-to-face with Christ's gospel and lead them to take up a definite position for or against the imperatives of this gospel. The Church has been sent out to bring men salvation, not a state of moral coma or a comfortable somnolence. This is her prophetic role; like John the Baptist, she is a voice in the desert, the messenger of God's rule and Christ's salvation. And, like John the Baptist, her message cannot always be a soothing lullaby.

We are sent out to make disciples 'of all the nations'. There is no explicit mention here of individuals, but rather of peoples and human groups. Obviously, we reach them only through the individual members, but there can be a distinction of orientation. Does not the phrase 'make disciples of all the nations' presume that missionaries will direct their attention to groups as such, and strive to reach them as communities—in their collective religious, cultural and social dimensions? Peoples, as groups or communities, must be seized by Christ and the Christian spirit; Christ must come to life in them, become a living presence and a new incarnation. Our task is not merely to proclaim Christ and his good news, but to incarnate Christ anew in a race, a people—in its culture, its thought and its whole mentality. Therefore we must constantly search for methods of proclaiming the gospel that will touch a responsive chord in a given tribe or people, in order to incarnate Christ in them. This is a most important part of the concept of 'missionary adaptation'. It will often mean leaving aside much of the 'western' aspect of the Church's history and tradition, so that we may more easily assimilate a new people into Christ's family. Before we can make them disciples they must be able to feel that Christ and his Church have come to visit them; they must be able to feel at home with the new revelation we bring.

We are also ordered to 'baptise them . . .'. Baptism is pre-eminently the sacrament of reconciliation and peace with God. It creates a new salvific situation, one which holds all the rich content of the traditional Israelite greeting: Shalom. 'Shalom', as used in the Old Testament, signifies much more than the absence of war; it is the state of total well-being that follows from man's peace with God, with his neighbour and within himself. And, as Christ was at pains to point out, only God can grant this complete peace—the world is powerless to achieve it. One of the objects of missionary activity is to bring this peace and reconciliation to men.

Missionary activity, then, is more than a set of pastoral duties; it is an attempt to take hold of man in his totality and the world in its totality in order to lead both of them to peace and unity. By the saving sacrament of baptism the Church reconciles men to their Maker and leads them into a redeemed world, and thus takes the first necessary step towards reconciling men and nations to one another. Peace with God is the only sound basis on which peace between men can be built. From this point of view, missionary work and its salvific function correspond precisely to the most ardent aspirations of our age—peace between nations and the unity of mankind.

Perhaps this can throw some light on the difficult question of the relation between missionary activity and development. As Pope Paul has put it, 'development is the new name for peace'. Development work, properly understood, is directed essentially to the service of peace and the unification of men, and with these aims should form an integral part of apostolic activity.

Promise: 'And know that I am with you always; yes, to the end of time.' Every missionary knows in his heart that he has taken on a task far too big for him to accomplish. But this is never a reason for despair, because he is not asked to perform the missionary task alone. The promise of Christ stands firm, and the miracle of Pentecost is renewed every time a frail man finds light and strength to lead his brother onward towards their common Father. This promise of Matthew 28 is but a deepening, a Christianisation, of a consistent Old Testament theme—God's enduring presence to his people, in trial and triumph. Christ and the Spirit he sends will always remain the force which animates and sustains the missionary. The whole narrative of the Acts of the Apostles shows that missionary activity is an operation dominated by the risen Christ and guided in its details by his Spirit. And this results in one of the fundamental laws of missionary endeavour: the leading of people and nations to God is not a work that relies for success on human techniques. We are humble ministers of Christ's charity to our fellow-men. It is for our Master to choose the place, the moment and the manner in which his kingdom will take root and grow. We move forward, as Paul did, in constant wonder before the mystery of God's action and our own instrumentality, and ever conscious, as he was, that salvation comes from God alone.

Every missionary is a delegate of Christ, and his delegation, as well as the spiritual force which sustains him and urges him on, is an essential part of the power of lordship which Christ exercises as *Kyrios*. And this power, which tends of its nature towards his second coming at the Parousia, gives an eschatological dimension to all missionary activity. This comes through very clearly, for example, in Mark 13:10: 'the Good News must first be proclaimed to all the nations'. The universal preaching of the Good News constitutes a necessary prelude to the Parousia, which is really the full and final establishment of God's kingdom—on earth and in heaven. It is obvious, especially from St Paul, that the period between Christ's ascension and his re-appearance at the Parousia is precisely the period of universal proclamation of his lordship. This is, in fact, our only real way of preparing for Christ's return as universal Lord. Literally, like John the Baptist, we prepare a way for the Lord, we make his paths straight. Missionary endeavour is the active and constructive expression of the Christian's hope in his Lord's return.

iii) *The Expanding Church*

Although not one of the Twelve, and even though having had no personal contact, as far as we know, with Christ, Paul never hesitated to call himself an apostle. He used the word at every possible opportunity; it became his standard introduction of himself: 'Paul, a servant of Jesus Christ who has been called to be an apostle' (*Rom.* 1:1). Just read the opening sentence of any of his letters to see how highly he valued the title 'apostle'. And we can hardly dispute his right to use it when we consider the similarity of his missionary mandate to that given to the original apostles: 'you are to be his witness before all mankind, testifying to what you have seen and heard' (*Acts* 22:15).

Happily we have outlived the era of exegesis that attempted to set Peter and Paul in theological opposition, Peter as the leader of a Palestinian group and Paul as the founder of a type of Christianity inspired by hellenistic tendencies and thus outward bound for the farthest reaches of the empire. Paul's missionary career, in fact, parallels that of his Master—he was an apostle first to the Jews and only then to the gentiles, as we have already seen.

We can never be sufficiently grateful to St Paul for his boundless energy. Missionaries in the field are not normally good correspondents, and we readily forgive the dearth of letters. But Paul, in spite of being a tireless traveller and a practical, worried missionary (who, besides, worked to earn his living), still managed to leave us the great collection of letters to his young communities that remain as a source of spiritual strength and a theology of missions. And he wrote these in spite of much suffering and harassment from without, and the inevitable conflicts and growing pains from within the infant local churches. If one were to read only the Acts of the Apostles, one might conclude that, in spite of the worst attempts of the Judaisers who hounded Paul from city to city, the Church's journey from Jerusalem to Rome was one of calm progress; St Luke has the extraordinary capacity of conveying at all times serenity and enthusiasm. But when we read Paul's letters, written from the heat of the controversies that boiled around him, we see that the Church moved forward slowly, painfully, on a veritable Way of the Cross, like her Founder. In fact, both accounts are true; only the point of view is different. Humanly speaking, it is surprising that, against so many obstacles, the missionary movement of the growing Church got under way so rapidly and so successfully. At the same time, it would be unrealistic to suppose that the members of the young Christian communities could suddenly sink their differences of personality and background and become a unanimous brotherhood of charity. Many arguments and much heart-searching led to the decree of the Council of Jerusalem, freeing gentile converts to Christianity from the obligation to become Jews by circumcision first. Peter pronounced their Magna Carta: 'Remember, we believe that we are saved in the same way as they are: through the grace of the Lord Jesus' (*Acts* 15:11). Many painful personal confrontations, including one between Peter and Paul ('I opposed him to his face'—*Gal.* 2:11), were to follow before peace was established between the new Christians of different origins, and before Paul could write: '. . . there is no room for distinction between Greek and Jew, between the circumcised and the uncircumcised, or between barbarian and Scythian, slave and free man. There is only Christ: he is everything and he is in everything' (*Col.* 3:11).

Before we do Paul the rank injustice of saying no more about him, there are two declarations of his that demand mention. One is his panoramic view of salvation history, in which he expresses all his missionary ardour and hopes in a tissue of Old Testament citations.

> It can only be to God's glory, then, for you to treat each other in the same friendly way as Christ treated you. The reason Christ became the servant of circumcised Jews was not only so that God could faithfully carry out the

promises made to the patriarchs, it was also to get the
pagans to give glory to God for his mercy, as scripture
says in one place: For this I shall praise you among the
pagans and sing to your name. And in another place:
Rejoice, pagans, with his people, and in a third place: Let
all the pagans praise the Lord, let all the peoples sing his
praises. Isaiah too has this to say: The root of Jesse will
appear, rising up to rule the pagans, and in him the
pagans will put their hope. May the God of hope bring
you such joy and peace in your faith that the power of the
Holy Spirit will remove all bounds to hope (*Rom.*
15:7–13).

The second is one of Paul's most profound statements, his
view of the ultimate *raison d'être* of apostolic effort:

> He has let us know the mystery of his purpose,
> the hidden plan he so kindly made in Christ from the
> beginning
> to act upon when the times had run their course to the end:
> that he would bring everything together under Christ,
> as head,
> everything in the heavens and everything on earth.
>
> (*Eph.* 1:9–10).

As chronologically the last and theologically the greatest of
the New Testament writers, John deserves more attention than
we can give him here. He is the only evangelist who does not
have a version of the missionary mandate at the end of his
gospel—but then he does not relate the institution of the
Eucharist either. John had lived and prayed through the early
struggles of the Church, had suffered the first fury of persecu-
tion, and had anguished over the first heresies to infect the
Mystical Body. And then he wrote his gospel. There is scant

space given to details; John's thought is high and theological. His gospel contains little that could be called specifically missionary, but has all through it a warm universalism based firmly on the inexhaustible love of God, John's insistent theme. His reaction to the turbulent decades through which he had lived, and to the struggles of the young missionary Church, is best expressed in 16:33: 'In the world you will have trouble, but be brave: I have conquered the world.'

To conclude this section, and this rapid survey of the biblical evidence, what answer can we now give to the question from which we originally set out: Why the missions? To quote Fr Schutte:

> Missions are necessary because of the revelation of the eschatological sovereignty of God among the peoples which was inaugurated by Christ. They are necessary because of Christ's request to make disciples of all nations. Missions are necessary because of the salvific function of the Church for reconciliation and peace, for a world one and saved, unified and at peace. Missions are necessary for the growth of the body of Christ and because of the love by which all the members of this body become aware, in the Holy Spirit, of their responsibility to communicate the life and the love of God to all men. Missions are necessary because they flow from the very being and inner nature of the Church.

PART II

Didache, Development and the Future

6 Salvation and Non-Christian Religions

Having given, in Part I, an outline of the theological and biblical basis of our missionary apostolate, it is time to turn to some of the specific problems which at present seem to threaten the traditional missionary urgency and dynamism. Of these, the crucial one is that of salvation outside the Church, or the salvific value of non-Christian religions. The reason is obvious: the necessity of membership of the visible Church for salvation has been one of the main driving forces of apostolic activity all through the centuries of the Church's expansion. Now that the values of other religions are being examined and emphasised, many missionaries are confused and in doubt. If the people to whom he has come are already, unaided, 'anonymous Christians', Christians in disguise, then has the missionary really a function to perform? The confusion is compounded by the discovery, easily made, that contradictory statements on this subject are sometimes made by the same theological school of thought. Perhaps more than any other area of theological investigation at present, this whole question is being bedevilled by a type of writing which presents an incautious and often bizarre mixture of truths of faith, genuine theological conclusions, and the temporary experimental private opinions and researches of theologians. One can understand and sympathise with a renowned theologian's exasperated comment on this subject at the symposium: 'We are tired of the repetition of utter nonsense by some modern theologians.'

While it has taken a more acute form in the past few years,

this is not by any means a new problem. Its roots go back to a very definite tension between two truths of faith, both of them explicitly stated in the Bible and repeated forcefully by the teaching Church. On the one hand, God 'wants everyone to be saved and reach full knowledge of the truth' (1 *Tim.* 2:4); on the other, 'no one knows the Father except the Son and those to whom the Son chooses to reveal him' (*Matt.* 11:27).

We have already spoken, in chapter 3, of the universal salvific will of God. Always a basic datum of ecclesiastical teaching, the universal salvific will of the Father and the universal redemptive will of the Son became, especially during the Jansenist period, the subject of a series of pronouncements by the Church's magisterium. Missionary activity has always been understood as a high form of charity specifically at the service of this universal salvific and redemptive divine will. This was Paul's view also: 'We are fellow workers with God; you are God's farm, God's building' (1 *Cor.* 3:9). Christ gave his missionary mandate to the Church, and so the Church sends out missionaries. And they have gone out with the intention of drawing men within her saving embrace. Thus, the universality of the divine will and the earthly universality of the Church have generally been accepted as aspects of the same movement of men towards the Parousia. But in this case, how do we explain the comparatively limited progress of the Church towards universal extension?

The tension between these two aspects was by no means reduced by Vatican II. Even more strongly than in documents of earlier centuries the universal salvific will is proclaimed anew. And side by side with that, the necessity of the Church for salvation is stoutly affirmed. The possibility of salvation for those who have no contact with the Church is acknowledged, but, side by side with that, the urgency of the Church's missionary task is stressed. The dilemma continues; it is sufficient to read articles 14–17 of *Lumen Gentium*. When the Church herself solemnly announced that men can receive salvation, even though they have no knowledge of the Church, the gospel or even of a personal God, some felt that apostolic zeal had been sapped at its source. It will not be too difficult to show that this is not so.

The carefully weighed words of *Lumen Gentium* are based on the theological growth and development of the concepts of revelation, salvation and the Church as People of God.

It is not possible to limit God's revelation of himself strictly to the confines of the biblical revelation in Old Testament and New. First, we have no right to set bounds to divine self-revealing; besides, it is obvious from the biblical evidence that God did not restrict the proofs of his love to Israel alone. We have already mentioned the significant fact that the first covenant recorded in the Old Testament is between God and all the family of man—Genesis 9. This covenant must have involved, at the very least, some knowledge of God, and an acceptance of his sovereignty over man and universe, and of his good intentions towards men. In other words, it presumes the minimum requirements for an approach to God as given in Hebrews 11:6: 'Now it is impossible to please God without faith, since anyone who comes to him must believe that he exists and rewards those who try to find him.'

That this knowledge of the true God continued, to some degree or other, among the 'nations' after the call of Abraham and the election of Israel is suggested by the occasional later appearances of pagans who seemed to acknowledge the lordship of Israel's God and to follow, at least partially, his signposts towards a correctly ordered human life. Melchizedek, Balaam, Ruth and Job we have mentioned in chapter 4. Many more names could be added; for example, Cyrus, the Persian monarch who conquered Babylon in 539 B.C., and one of whose first acts was to allow the exiled Jews to return to Jerusalem. And not merely did he allow them to go; he encouraged and helped them—Ezra 1. Deutero-Isaiah calls Cyrus God's 'shepherd' and his 'anointed'—Isaiah 45.

In the wisdom literature, mostly written at the end of the Old Testament period, the concept of some true knowledge of God—'wisdom'—in peoples outside the sphere of Israel's special revelation occurs several times. Ecclesiasticus, in his great hymn to the wonders of man, makes no distinction between Jew and gentile.

> He filled them with knowledge and understanding,
> and revealed to them good and evil.
> He put his own light in their hearts
> to show them the magnificence of his works (*Eccles.* 17:7-8).

In the New Testament, Christ pointed to a pagan, a Roman centurion, and told his Jewish audience: 'I tell you solemnly, nowhere in Israel have I found faith like this' (*Matt.* 8:10). Several times St Paul insists, in no uncertain terms, that many of the evils of paganism spring from conscious rejection of divine gifts and illuminations received; for example: 'In particular, I want to urge you in the name of the Lord, not to go on living the aimless kind of life that pagans live. Intellectually they are in the dark, and they are estranged from the life of God, without knowledge because they have shut their hearts to it' (*Eph.* 4:17-18). Romans 1:18-32 is a meditation on this very theme.

What conclusions can we draw from all this? This is terrain in which exegetical exaggeration seems to flourish readily. In Romans 1, for example, Paul is merely repeating the argumentation of Wisdom 13—that men can reasonably be expected to deduce the existence of God from the created things about them, and to gather some ideas about him, 'his everlasting power and deity'. But can this be called in any sense a revelation, or is it simply a normal exercise of reason? Many theologians argue that it is more than the latter, and use different titles to describe it—illumination, natural revelation, cosmic revelation. Its origin, they hold, is certainly God, but we can only speculate on the means he employs to convey it to men—perhaps a vague interior enlightenment, perhaps a prophetic understanding of the created universe. It is something more than a natural knowledge based on creation—a theodicy: it is rather a divine impulse prompting men to discern, behind the forces and rhythms of nature, a benevolent Providence and eventually a loving Father. But, even granting this cosmic revelation, it is immediately clear that the elements of knowledge of God that it is capable of giving are few and fragmentary. And it is a very poor thing indeed when contrasted with the full splendour of the Christian revelation.

In talking on the subject: Revelation and Salvation outside the visible Church, Fr Semmelroth summarised the contemporary theological understanding of these terms. A long-accepted definition of salvation sees it as a reality achieved by God in men, and communicated to men by the work of Christ. By this grace, which the New Testament calls justification or eternal life, men are transformed into what St Paul calls a new creature: 'It does not matter if a person is circumcised or not; what matters is for him to become an altogether new creature' (*Gal.* 6:15). This view of salvation is not incorrect, but it needs to be complemented by taking account of the human element. What God reveals to man is essentially God himself, and by this man is enabled to live in what we may call a state of meeting with God, which is a sharing in the meeting of Son with Father in the unity of the holy Spirit, and is identified by the prayer: Abba, Father. 'The proof that you are sons is that God has sent the Spirit of his Son into our hearts: the Spirit that cries, "Abba, Father" ' (*Gal.* 4:6). Salvation is realised, then, in a union which is based on a continuing process of personal encounter between God and man. Man is never a purely passive object of the divine activity; he must offer his own personal response.

Similarly, the traditional understanding of the nature and

meaning of revelation did not convey the full richness of the concept. Revelation was considered to have one function only —to communicate a knowledge of supernatural truths. Without these, man could not make a personal decision for or against God. In other words, revelation had to come before salvation. It was within such limitations that Vatican I interpreted divine revelation. Thus there is a considerable advance in the treatment of Vatican II. It complements the older philosophico-theological idea and presents revelation, not as a preparation for salvation, but as an integral part of the accomplishing of salvation. In his salvific action God reveals himself to men, in such a way that they are rendered capable of a community of life with God. God gives men, by the fact that he reveals himself to them, the capacity to open themselves in turn to him, in a real association and dialogue. Thus, revelation is not merely a set of instructions about salvation, but belongs to the salvation process itself. Revelation is not merely the words of God but also the actions of God. 'This plan of revelation is realised by deeds and words having an inner unity; the deeds wrought by God in the history of salvation manifest and confirm the teaching and realities signified by the words, while the words proclaim the deeds and clarify the mystery contained in them. By this revelation then, the deepest truth about God and the salvation of man is made clear to us in Christ, who is the Mediator and at the same time the fullness of all revelation'—*Dei Verbum* (On Divine Revelation), article 2.

God, in revealing himself as salvation, calls men in an intimately personal way, not in abstract or exclusively intellectual terms. And this call is not something set outside of salvation but is an essential part of it. The call itself reveals God, and men, in responding to this call, surrender themselves to God and to a community of life with God. Divine truth is a gift that only God can give, but men do not possess it as something of their own; rather they are possessed by it.

In the light of this, where does the Church enter the salvation process? And what is our reaction now to that long-suffering axiom: *extra Ecclesiam nulla salus*? We have a right to ask: is this statement still true or not? If true, precisely how is it to be understood? In attempting an answer to these questions, it is necessary to put the phrase in historical perspective; like many axioms, it has suffered, for most of its history, from interpretations that were too simplistic and too literal.

A phrase of this kind normally becomes immortal because it expresses a truth with the minimum of words and the maximum dramatic impact. The credit for being the author of *'extra Ecclesiam nulla salus'* goes to St Cyrian, bishop of Carthage in the first half of the third century. And the phrase was born during a stormy conflict in the North African church. The followers of men who had openly broken with the Church and gladly accepted the stigma of 'heretic', like Valentinus and Marcion, continued to administer the sacrament of baptism. Were such sacraments valid or not? Cyprian held strongly that they could not be, and argued thus: only the Church, as the Spouse of Christ, can give birth to children of God. In order to have God for their Father, men must have the Church for their Mother. Only in the Church can salvation be achieved. How then can there be a valid baptism outside the Church?

In spite of the partially false conclusion and the negative line of argument, Cyprian had taken his stand on a positive element of fundamental Christian teaching: God had given salvation to the world by Christ; Christ had prolonged his salvific function by means of the Church. Thus, in the Church, and only in the Church, was salvation to be achieved.

The axiom lived and gathered strength through constant and official ecclesiastical repetition. The necessity of the Church for salvation was taught—always citing Cyprian's happy phrase—by a whole succession of Church Councils. And it was accepted quite literally and with no qualification by some, for example the Council of Florence, which goes on to quote approvingly the extreme position of Fulgentius: 'Not only pagans but also Jews, heretics and schismatics will have no share in eternal life. They will go into the eternal fire which was prepared for the devil and his angels, unless they become aggregated to the Catholic Church before the end of their lives.' However, since the time of Pius IX, some of the necessary qualifications began to be added explicitly—those who live in invincible ignorance of the Christian religion can be saved by God. This progress culminated in the letter of the Holy Office to the then Archbishop Cushing of Boston in 1949, refuting the Harvard teaching of Father Feeney, who had insisted that salvation was possible only by explicit membership of the Catholic Church.

However, while the facts were slowly growing in clarity, the explanation of them underwent many variations and vicissitudes. Few theologians expressed complete satisfaction with the 'categories': members of the Church *in re* and *in voto*; those attached to the 'body' of the Church and to the 'soul' of the Church. The main objection was that these were strictly juridical categories, and as such incapable of taking full account of the variety of personal approaches of men to God and vice versa.

What, in the present state of theological opinion, is the meaning of the axiom? First, an obvious remark. The principle was proposed in definite historical circumstances—with reference to apostates who, having full knowledge of the Church, set themselves up against her. Only later was the phrase used in a more general sense to indicate all outside the Church. Therefore it must be applied with care when we are talking about men who have no ill-will towards the Church but who are in involuntary ignorance of her existence or her nature.

The evidence of Scripture is ample to show that the only way to salvation is Christ. And Christ founded his Church to prolong and expand his saving influence on men. Therefore, not merely are men obliged to seek salvation through the Church, but God has obliged himself, within our understanding of his salvation plan, to lead men to him by and through his Church. Thus we must affirm, without hesitation, that the normal and indispensable means of salvation is the Church, in its divine origin and its historical unfolding. At the same time, God's universal plan for man's salvation is both older and wider than the Church. And obviously the Church cannot, and does not wish to, either limit God's saving presence or exhaust God's saving grace. But when we refer to non-Christian religions, it is important not to regard them as anti-Christian religions; they must be understood and evaluated with reference to the Church, not as necessarily in opposition to the Church.

In saying this we are not proposing that non-Christian religions are the same as Christianity, which is, by divine, public, positive institution, an official activity of God in the world. Nor are we proposing that non-Christian religions are parallel to Christianity, as if all of them were roads leading to the Father with equal security and directness. It is an exaggeration, even if a fashionable one in some circles, to say that these religions are 'ordinary' or normal means of salvation. This is to go far beyond the statements of Vatican II.

Now, let's try to look a little more closely at the non-Christian religions themselves, following the approach of Cardinal Daniélou in his paper at the symposium. Here we are concerned with the religions as such, not with individual members of these religions. That means that we are talking about recognisable social religious institutions or groups, each possessing its own complex of doctrines, obligations and rites. All religions represent an authentic religious experience, and this finds expression in various forms, for example, the sacralisation of the fundamental rhythms of human life—birth, marriage, death—mainly through rites.

However, side by side with these authentic values, these religions are human creations, and thus liable to many deformations. It would be absurd to say that all natural religion is idolatry, but it is nevertheless a fact that a particular interpretation of the sacred character of nature, which is a sign of God, can and does occasionally degenerate into idolatry. The same is true of magic. The rites of pagan religions are not in themselves magic rites. But sometimes they are perverted into sheer magic. Besides, pagan mysticism remains always an uncertain quest, because the God that it seeks is, by definition, beyond its reach. That is why the image it forms of this God is often distorted. This explains the disparity we sometimes find, especially in eastern religions, between the heroic virtues of their great thinkers and the discordant and disappointing content of the message they transmitted.

The Judæo-Christian revelation puts us in the presence of an entirely different situation. Religion testifies to man's incessant search for a transcendent God. Revelation shows us the free decision by which God, in an unexpected and unmerited act of love, finds man and shows himself to man. The abyss between Creator and creature could not be bridged by man, and so God himself bridged it. This gesture of divine affection is, strictly speaking, salvation. As we have seen, this reality is encountered outside and apart from biblical revelation, but the uniqueness of the biblical revelation is that salvation has been granted to men. Salvation, in the context of its biblical history, is not merely something possible, but something objectively accomplished.

It is not religion, of any kind, that saves men; only Christ saves them. Any man who is saved, no matter which religion he embraces, is saved by Christ and by Christ alone. But how then does this salvation, whose only source is Christ, come to men who do not know Christ? Or, to put the same question in another way, what is required for salvation in the case of a man who has no knowledge of the redemptive act accomplished once for all by Christ? Paul answers this question in Romans, where he says that the Jew will be judged according to the Law and the pagan according to his conscience. 'Sinners who were not subject to the Law will perish all the same, without that Law; sinners who were under the Law will have that Law to judge them' (*Rom.* 2:12). This is another way of saying that every man will be judged according to the knowledge of God that is available to him.

What happens when we apply this standard to non-Christian religions? As we have seen, these religions are human creations, organisations of an authentic religious feeling and impulse. Since they are human creations, they share the fate of a humanity which, left to itself, so easily mixes truth and error. Their authority is human, not divine. There is always to be found in them a deep and disturbing ambiguity. They are forms through which the people of a particular civilisation express their religious experiences, but they can present a distorted vision of the experience and thus constitute an obstacle to true progress towards God.

Missionary tradition has been quite correct in recognising, in pagan religions, both stepping-stones and stumbling-blocks. Thus it would be far too optimistic to consider non-Christian religions purely and simply as the ordinary means of salvation for those who do not know Christ. They are marked by sin, as is everything in man not purified and guided by Christ. It would be a grave practical error to conclude that the members of these religions are in such a relationship to salvation that our missionary obligations toward them are less urgent than our predecessors had believed. But our approach to them must be based on a soundly Christian combination of deep respect and healthy realism.

It would be helpful and consoling if we had more information on how other religions provide the possibility of salvation to their members. But in this sphere we can only speculate and propound theories, because this is a mystery of God's love. Still, it may be helpful to look at some of the prevailing theological theories about how non-Christians find God and salvation.

But first, can we answer a general question: do they find salvation *in* their religions, *through* their religions, or *in spite of* their religions? Unconvinced by the arguments of the 'dialectic' theologians, it is both unjust and unduly pessimistic to say: 'in spite of' their religions. We have tried to show that there is a genuine stretching out towards God in all religious forms, and God has guaranteed to reward and rescue all who sincerely seek him. Are they then saved 'through' their religions? Following the careful wording of *Lumen Gentium*, article 16, it seems necessary to answer: No. 'Whatever goodness or truth is found among them is looked upon by the Church as a preparation for the gospel. She regards such qualities as given by Him who enlightens all men so that they may finally have life.' The ambiguous character of these religions and the defects inherent in their structures and signs warn us against describing them too simply as 'channels of grace'. At best, they are the milieu of Christ's grace and salvation. After all, not even a Christian is saved by Christianity as a religion, but by Jesus Christ, the unique Saviour. 'For of all the names in the world given to men, this is the only one by which we can be saved' (*Acts* 4:12).

Therefore non-Christians can be saved 'in' their own religions; it is within the framework of these religions that God's grace reaches them. Men do not live in isolation, but as members of a given social group and members of a given religion, and these factors have an influence on their formation. Thus, God's salvific will implies that his grace reaches men in their life-situation, and thus in their religions. In spite of errors and aberrations, these religions propose a modicum of truth and indicate an orientation towards God and an incipient God-man relationship. On these foundations the mercy and providence of God can build.

We can mention briefly four of the current theories about how non-Christians find salvation, emphasising again that here we are exclusively in the sphere of speculation.

The oldest of these, and still widely accepted, is that in these religions men conceive an implicit desire for membership of the Church, or implicit acceptance of the Church as the divinely appointed road to God. But two reservations must be made. In the new glow of ecumenism, this viewpoint sounds offensively triumphalistic both to our fellow-Christians and to non-Christians. Again, perhaps it would be wiser—and closer to the truth—to focus this implicit desire on Christ rather than on the Church. It is correct that the way to meet Christ is through his Church. But the Church is not the centre of salvation history; this is exclusively the risen Christ, the Lord of history and the author of salvation.

Gaining ground strongly at present is the theory of the fundamental option, or act of commitment. The fundamental option is the basic act of will by which a man fundamentally directs his whole life to God. It is, in fact, the same idea as the biblical 'metanoia', which must be understood as a change in the direction of one's life. A man can either shut himself up in selfish love and refuse the 'others', both God and men, or he can open himself out in selfless love, accepting his own existence and situation and thereby accepting God and other men as part of his life's pattern. In this openness to the various aspects of his life, in this spirit of love, service and acceptance of others there is an implicit act of faith. It is a response to a divine invitation; it is a 'Yes' and an 'Amen' to God's intervention in his existence and in the history of mankind. And by this he is saved.

But how precisely do non-Christian religions contribute towards leading men to this fundamental option? Here is the viewpoint of an Indian theologian, Fr Amalorpavadass, whose paper at the symposium we shall mention several times again. Within the Church, the grace of Christ reaches us by words and signs, by the gospel and the Eucharist, which are all differing aspects of the one basic sacrament—the Church. These signs of Christianity were instituted by God, endowed with significance and efficacity, and continue because of the continuing presence of Christ. Sacraments are actions of Christ because they signify various historical salvation events, and they re-enact these realities today for those who believe in them. Are there any corresponding means provided by God for the salvation of non-Christians in their own religions?

God acts normally through the physical and historical order—he uses signs which are natural and ordinary. So we must ask if the signs, the rites of other religions are salvific. Again, signs are never efficacious by themselves. They become efficacious and salvific only if they refer to the God beyond them, and precisely as the God who comes to save man. But often non-Christian religions lack even the concept of creation and personal God—and what then becomes of their signs? However, there is an important distinction to be made here. If we consider, for example, Hinduism, as a religious system and structure, its elements are ritualistic and closed in upon themselves. But if we watch Hindus at their religious exercises, listen to their moving cries for mercy and forgiveness and their heartfelt prayers of adoration, love and surrender, we hesitate to brand all these as superstitious or magical acts. On the other hand, when we observe some Christians at their devotions or even receiving the sacraments, we wonder if they do not live in a world of rituals with little understanding of their true significance, with almost no reference to the Person of Christ. Thus in individual cases and persons, the signs of Hinduism, though not salvific in themselves, may become genuinely prophetic, and open on to a personal God and a response to his interventions and invitations.

Another suggestion for the relationship between members of other religions and the Church is put forward by the German theologian Muhlen. He starts from a new viewpoint on the Church: the Church is not so much the continuation of the incarnation as the continuation of Christ's anointing by the holy Spirit. In fact, he defines the Church as the mystery of the identity of the holy Spirit in Christ and Christians, or the mystery of one Person in many persons.

Christ's anointing by the holy Spirit had two distinct aspects, which can be called the aspect of sanctification and the aspect of consecration. The holy Spirit first sanctified the humanity Christ had assumed, and then consecrated him, or ordained him to his messianic office. By virtue of the salvific brotherhood of Christ and Christians, the same two functions of sanctification and consecration are verified in the life of every Christian. By the sanctifying unction of the holy Spirit, the Christian receives the Spirit for his own salvation; by the consecratory anointing of the Spirit, he is constituted an official mediator of God's grace for the benefit of others. The Church, as continuing to the end of time the anointing of Christ by the Spirit, must faithfully preserve and reproduce these two functions of the Spirit. While the sanctificatory aspect could be (and is) verified in an 'invisible' Church, the consecratory aspect requires visibility and the capacity to be recognised as an authentic messianic activity in the world—as a divinely anointed and sacramental community in the Spirit. Muhlen sees this as the essential difference between the invisible or anonymous Christian and the baptised member of the visible Church. The former has received only a sanctifying anointing by the Spirit— he has genuinely been touched by God and has received a gift of the Spirit which can lead him to the Father and the Son. The living member of the Church, on the other hand, has been both sanctified and consecrated by the Spirit; he is not merely on the path to salvation but is a sacrament of salvation to others, a visible and audible agent of God's life-giving Spirit to the world.

Finally, there is the 'representation' or 'substitution' theory, possibly the most promising of them all. While this may be rather far removed from contemporary pragmatic thought, it has the great advantage of being a soundly biblical idea. Since the Church continues Christ and his saving work in the world, obviously she must exercise the function of representative before God on behalf of men. The Church is not a mechanical distributor of the fruits of Christ's passion; following in the footsteps of her Master, she presents herself humbly as a representative before God, not merely of her own members but also of those who do not know her and even of these who oppose her. She too has to repeat the words of the tortured Christ: 'Father, forgive them; they do not know what they are doing' (*Luke* 23:34). And we, as members of the Church, must take this duty seriously—it is an essential part of our ministry to non-Christians. We must never be satisfied to reap the benefits of membership of the Church without shouldering its obligations. One is reminded of the great phrase of de Lubac: 'The City of the Elect does not welcome profiteers.' The Church was never intended to be a group of the smugly self-centred 'saved'—even though there are sects with this peculiar outlook—but rather a community called together in order to be at the service of all.

Whichever theory we prefer, we must still bow in humility before the goodness of God and the mysterious ways in which this goodness is at work, far outside the visible framework of Christ's Church. It is useless to look for proofs or signs—we must only be grateful that God's mercy knows no limits. But surely one of the constant and comforting signs of his salvific action is the simple piety and goodness of heart that we can find in areas where no Christian revelation has penetrated. Fr Fransen, S.J., has written:

Let us think of the sincere love and dedication of millions of poor and humble people, who cannot penetrate deeply into the problems of religion, and will probably have nothing to offer to God but this love at the moment of their death. I have in mind, for example, the kind and simple people of India, whose inner life, while it must remain unknown to this world, is known to God and his Spirit. They have neither the time nor the ability to think very deeply about the problems of faith and religion. Following their conscience and the discreet invitation of grace, they can only remain true to the religious traditions of their ancestors, as long as the Christian faith has not illuminated their conscience, entering into their lives as Christ very kindly and patiently entered into the lives of the Galilean peasants, shepherds and fishermen. Christianity in the meantime is still for most of them a foreign religion which they cannot understand, because it still does not belong to their ordinary life in the villages. From their own traditions they spontaneously retain the more simple and popular forms of devotion, frequently mixed with superstition and coarse religious practices. But they know of no better form of religion which might appeal to them. Yet Christ died for them as for us, and he is already sending his Spirit into their hearts. The Spirit of Christ is attracting them towards a greater love for their fellow-men in their families and villages. Whenever they listen to his voice and follow the supernatural impulse of grace, they may encounter God in the sincerity of their love for their neighbours and brothers.

To conclude: non-Christian religions have a place within God's universal salvation plan, because they contain authentic spiritual values which are the fruits of God's presence and activity. The followers of these religions come within God's salvific will, but how his will and his graces reach and save them—or how many of them—we have no way of knowing.

What message does all this carry for the missionary? We hope to see this in more detail in the following chapter, but this much must be said now. It is necessary to be cautious about exaggerated statements and unfounded optimism. Christianity is a religion of a completely different order from all others. It is not an expression of a human search for God; it is the result of God's search for man—a divine historical event with results that no man can ignore. As Cardinal Daniélou has said: 'It would be absurd for an African to adopt an Indian religion, or for an Oceanian to adopt an Arab religion. One should have the religion of one's race, tradition and nation.' But Christianity is the voice of a universal Lord, who came into the world to bring all, African and Arab, to the feet of his Father. It has nothing to do with a man's nation, but it does contain his true destiny. There is no question, therefore, of equality of religions, or parallelism of religions; and God's universal charity does not in any way impose frontiers on his universal missionary mandate. It is important to remember that 1 Timothy 2:4 not only says that God 'wants everyone to be saved' but also that he wants them to 'reach full knowledge of the truth'. The great central truth for all men is, and will ever be, that the Son of God died to save them and rose to glorify them. And those who are blessed to know this will always wish to share it with those who do not.

It is significant that Vatican II was silent on the methods by which God leads men to himself. It passed no judgement on the venerable axiom, *extra Ecclesiam . . .* , but did express a similar thought more positively; the Church is 'the universal sacrament of salvation' (*Lumen Gentium*, art. 48). And it said nothing which would justify us automatically calling non-Christians 'anonymous Christians'.

Vatican II does say that the goodness and truth to be found—

and abundantly—in non-Christian religions are certainly 'a preparation for the gospel' (*Lumen Gentium*, art. 16). In other words, the Council was faithful to the thought of St Paul, for whom Christ was all in all, thanks to his own conversion, his experiences in the young Christian communities and his deep, long and prayerful meditations on his Lord's death and resurrection. For Paul, who remains the norm for every Christian missionary, to preach Christ was the greatest privilege he could enjoy, and the greatest favour he could bestow on the sophisticated Roman empire. Has this situation changed since? We, as missionaries, are still 'stewards entrusted with the mysteries of God' (1 *Cor.* 4:1); the gospel is still the 'power of God saving all who have faith' (*Rom.* 1:16).

Therefore the urgency of our missionary task remains; in fact, the urgency increases, as we notice our inability to keep pace with the population growth, and as we recall that non-Christians of all kinds need us. They are, as Scripture and Council assure us, in a state of being 'towards Christ', but they are not yet 'in Christ'; and as long as they are not, we have work to do—and so much of it. As missionaries, we still must carry the Good News, the only really good news there is in this world burdened by catastrophe, cold war, strikes and suicides. And when we convey this good news to our little audience, we are not merely uncovering hidden Christians—as is suggested by some whose charity may have outrun their cerebration—we are creating new Christians, and we do so with all the joy of St Paul: 'it was I who begot you in Christ Jesus by preaching the Good News' (1 *Cor.* 4:15).

7 Evangelisation and Religious Freedom

The new and more Christian attitude to followers of other religions may appear to some as an obstacle to, or at least a brake on, missionary activity in the traditional sense. When we add to this the teaching of Vatican II on religious freedom, the combination can provoke a real dilemma for the missionary. *Dignitatis Humanae* (Declaration on Religious Freedom) says quite strongly: 'This freedom means that all men are to be immune from coercion on the part of individuals or of social groups and of any human power, in such wise that in matters religious no one is to be forced to act in a manner contrary to his own beliefs. Nor is anyone to be restrained from acting in accordance with his own beliefs, whether privately or publicly, whether alone or in association with others, within due limits' (art. 2). When we translate these words into practice, are we, in effect, tying the missionary's hands? Can it be that his preaching of the Christian faith to pagans or Muslims or Buddhists is a violation of their freedom, that he is putting unacceptable pressure on their consciences and disturbing their existing good faith? These are serious questions, and deserve a closer look.

First, let us be quite clear about what Vatican II does say. 'The Synod further declares that the right to religious freedom has its foundation in the very dignity of the human person, as this dignity is known through the revealed Word and by reason itself' (*Dig. Hum.*, art. 2). Thus the ultimate basis for religious freedom is man's inherent dignity as a human person. This dignity results in both privileges and obligations: the privilege of acting on his own judgement and the obligation of assuming full responsibility for his actions or omissions. A man's religious decisions are inalienably his own—and his alone. They cannot be made for him; he must not be compelled to make them, nor restrained from making them. So religious freedom is not a special postulate of the Catholic faith—it is a postulate of humanity.

The Declaration on Religious Freedom continues: ' . . . every man has the duty, and therefore the right, to seek the truth in matters religious, in order that he may with prudence form for himself right and true judgements of conscience, with the use of all suitable means. Truth, however, is to be sought after in a manner proper to the dignity of the human person and his social nature. The inquiry is to be free, carried on with the aid of teaching or instruction, communication, and dialogue' (art. 3). The remainder of this chapter will be merely a commentary on this citation.

The true concept of religious liberty, then, is this: religious truth cannot be imposed on a man, by force or fear or fraud. Therefore civil society must give freedom of proclamation and of worship to all religions; the Council does not advocate a denominational or confessional State. And Vatican II claimed the right to religious freedom not merely for the Catholic Church but equally for all religions. In demanding this right the Church is not asking privileges from the civil powers; she asks only the right to propose the truth to men. The Church treasures Christ's fidelity to his promise that 'the truth will make you free' (*John* 8:32). She does not claim the right to *impose* her truth on men, but she does claim the freedom to *propose* it to all.

The practical consequences of all this for our task of evangelisation are far-reaching. Evangelisation means announcing, in concrete circumstances of time and place, the salvation of the individual and of man's history which has been achieved by

Christ. It is a message not merely eschatological but eschatolo-gising, that is, it not merely proclaims a message of hope, but actively turns man and history towards the ultimate terminus of their evolution—what the New Testament calls 'the king-dom of heaven'. This, however, does not mean that the message of salvation is 'evasive' for man—providing an escape from the pressures of life, the demands of others and the exigencies of social human living. It frees man, yes; but not in the aristocratic sense of lifting him above the normal historical circumstances of his culture and century. On the contrary, the gospel message finds man where he lives, at his particular point in the historical progression of humanity's hard climb upwards from cave to civilisation. Evangelisation brings to men not only the logical finale of this progress but the explanation of the whole journey. Thus it approaches man 'as he is', in his concrete historical, political, social, economic, cultural situation. The gospel is Good News for an individual in all these circumstances; it is not directed to an academic abstraction. Also, it brings to the individual man a message that has repercussions on all these elements of his life-situation and that equips him to deal with them more surely.

With this attitude as his point of departure, the Spanish theologian, Fr Gonzalez-Ruiz, went on to draw three con-clusions relevant to missionary work.

1. Missionaries have no right to violate either the individual or collective conscience by the imposition of evangelisation. To avoid even the appearance of imposition, it is important that the gospel message should not be too closely tied to any particular cultural, social or political entity. Perhaps we still have much to learn from the Acts of the Apostles in this regard. St Paul had to grapple with most of our missionary problems—and with much less tradition and preparation. But, with the aid of the Spirit, he steered a prudent if often painful path through a maze of pitfalls.

For instance, with clear-sighted determination he fought all his life long against the monopolist tendencies of the Judaeo-Christians. Men of goodwill were coming into the Church from vastly different origins: from Palestinian Judaism, from the Diaspora synagogues, from paganism of various kinds—and Paul resolutely refused to oblige any one of them to renounce the heritage of his original culture. When the Judaisers attempted to impose the specific Jewish obligation of circumcision on all converts, Paul held out, strongly and successfully, for what modern theological jargon would call 'the religious pluriformism of the gospel'. In general terms, he had to deal with two groups, called in his letters Jews and Greeks. The gospel could not identify itself with one or the other, and had no desire to suppress one or the other. Paul's superlative achievement was to welcome, accept and sublimate both into the new Christian way of life without thereby destroying their original specific differences.

As for Paul himself, he never forgot or rejected his Jewish heritage, and he never, in spite of much suffering at their hands, turned his back on his own people. 'Brothers, I have the very warmest love for the Jews, and I pray to God for them to be saved' (*Rom.* 10:1). He always respected the ancient venerable traditions of Israel, without, however, demanding that the 'Greeks' and the 'barbarians' observe them. Thus the gospel was incarnated in vastly different types of communities around the Mediterranean littoral, and this without losing any of its integrity and purity. The Christianity of the first three centuries presents a marvellous example of religious diversity in a completely Christian unity, a diversity which revealed itself chiefly in the extraordinary richness and variety of the oriental and western liturgies.

2. The Good News of salvation must be, and must be seen to be, freely given. 'You received without charge, give without charge' (*Matt.* 10:8). Individuals and peoples must receive the

gospel as a completely gratuitous gift, which God offers on his own initiative and independent of any merit of men. Thus, a potentially unhealthy situation is created whenever evangelisation is 'aided' by dependence on, or too close a connection with, foreign aid or political influence. Apart from all other considerations, historical experience has demonstrated that most human groups react by accepting the aid but despising the apparently related religious message.

3. Taking the lessons of history seriously, missionaries must preserve a prudent independence and avoid various seductive forms of 'imperialism' that can plague our apostolic efforts. A superiority complex, often unconscious, can be operative in several ways:

Historico-racial imperialism: the gospel is presented as the exclusive patrimony of a superior race, and is shared with others only as an act of condescension.

Socio-economic imperialism: the gospel makes its appearance in connection with a set of development projects, leaning heavily on the money of a wealthy 'mission-sending' country.

Political imperialism: the presence of missionaries in a given area assures their mother-country of a certain political advantage. This is mainly a mirage, of course.

Cultural imperialism: the missionaries import their foreign culture and customs and ignore those of their adopted country. There are historical records of missionaries in China who, in thirty years, never learned a word of Chinese.

Religious imperialism: missionaries do not really evangelise the religions they find, but abruptly jettison them and give the impression that they are substituting a 'western' religion.

Sensitive people—and it is always unwise to underestimate the sensitivity of others—are justified in interpreting any one of these attitudes as a direct attack on their religious liberty. The root of the trouble is that, in all these cases, the gospel message— of Christ and him crucified—is linked with entities to which it does not belong and with which it has no inherent association. And this does a grave injustice to the gospel itself, to the peoples for whom it is destined, and to the missionaries who bring it.

Obviously, these different forms of imperialism are not all to be found in any one missionary, nor are any of them to be found in most missionaries, but there are still traces of a patronising attitude and faint echoes of a happily vanished colonialism. The 'sundowner' on the verandah; the mission house safely tucked away from the noise and smells of the market-place, and guarded, as the mythical Englishman guards his castle, either by a big dog or a gruff manner; the office hours so scrupulously observed, and not apparently for the benefit of the people: these may be indications of a lingering 'colonial' attitude still hanging around some mission stations and episcopal residences—like cigar smoke in an empty room.

However, to be just to missionaries, who are usually adaptable and open to new ideas, it must be said that, aided by contemporary theology and psychology, and encouraged by the insights of Vatican II, they are now seriously seeking ways by which they can increase their apostolic effectiveness and present a more accurate vision of salvation. We do not need a theological investigation to determine our right to preach; the right and the duty come directly from Christ's mandate and the Church's mission, as we have attempted to show. But we should be, and are, in earnest search of new approaches that will enable us to propose a more telling version of the Christian kerygma and at the same time maintain a deep respect for the people we address and the religious beliefs to which they presently adhere.

In this whole area there are three key ideas which serve as reliable guidelines for action and signposts to a fruitful missionary future:

a proper appreciation of the message we carry;

a mentality that is thoroughly and modernly missionary;

a method of contact with people that is soundly Christian.

It is relatively easy for missionaries to underestimate the importance of their task and the nobility of their message. *Quotidiana vilescunt*—and we must frequently remind ourselves, in contemplation and in action, of the priceless treasure we carry. Matthew's collection of parables in chapter 13 contains exactly the right images to drive the point home, if we think about them long enough: the good seed, the yeast, the treasure, the pearl of great value. In practical terms, the missionary brings to all men both word and sacrament: the Good News of salvation and the saving rite of baptism. Nobody doubts or disputes this, but perhaps we may usefully pause to consider the relation between these two elements of the Christian message.

Our understanding of the correct relationship between word and sacrament has suffered from various shifts in emphasis during the historical development of our theology. To put it briefly, theological writing after the Council of Trent introduced an imbalance which is only now being redressed. Probably in reaction to the Reformation emphasis on faith, post-Tridentine theology upheld the necessity of sacraments, but to such an extent that the role of faith in their reception did not always receive the attention it deserved. Contemporary theology is trying to establish the true link between them, and, in the missionary context, our chief interest is in the relationship between faith and baptism as the means of entry into the Church.

The obvious starting-point for this inquiry must be the Acts of the Apostles. The missionary activity described in the Acts takes consistently the two forms of proclamation and baptism. That the two are intimately united becomes clear from even a cursory glance at the content of the kerygma itself. The preaching of the apostles has been preserved in a schematic form in the discourses recorded in the Acts, for example, chapters 2, 3, 10. From a comparison between them it emerges that the original catechesis consisted of: a) the presentation of the testimony—the witness given to the life, death, resurrection and glorification of Christ; b) the call to faith, repentance and baptism.

This constant joining of the sacrament of baptism to the primitive preaching can be satisfactorily explained only as obedience to a formal command of Christ. This is, of course, confirmed by the wording of the missionary mandate in Matthew and Mark, where proclamation and baptism are mentioned together as elements of evangelisation. Proclamation leads to faith in the person of Christ, and baptism, in Paul's magnificent insight, is immersion into the person of Christ. 'You have been taught that when we were baptised in Christ Jesus we were baptised in his death; in other words, when we were baptised we went into the tomb with him and joined him in death, so that as Christ was raised from the dead by the Father's glory, we too might live a new life' (*Rom.* 6:3–4). The whole New Testament testimony indicates that baptism is never separated from faith; it gives external expression to the inner union with God accomplished by faith. That is why Paul can ascribe the very same effects to both baptism and faith, as can be seen from a comparison between passages like Romans 6:3–9 (baptism) and Galatians 2:16–20 (faith).

Faith and baptism are really the two aspects, human and divine, of the new covenant. Man surrenders himself to God by faith, and God takes man into his friendship officially and publicly by the rite of baptism. To minimise the importance of one or the other is to impoverish the whole message. The missionary is the appointed bearer of both Good News and sacramental rite. Only when we missionaries appreciate this ourselves can we hope to have a true apostolic impulse—the desire to share with all men the riches of our own experience of God and our vision of his salvation plan.

This, in turn, will guide us towards a mentality that is thoroughly and modernly missionary. Helping ourselves to the wealth of ideas thrown out by Fr Amalorpavadass, we can mention, as among the component parts of such a mentality, what he calls a global vision, a historical perspective, and a sense of an incarnational economy.

It is possible that, occasionally at least, we have allowed ourselves to be preoccupied by individual conversions. But no individual can be either considered or approached in isolation, and Vatican II recalls us many times to the basic concept of the community of man. Men 'are formed into large and distinct groups by permanent cultural ties, by ancient religious traditions and by firm bonds of social necessity' (*Ad Gentes,* art. 10). Therefore we must learn to take account of men in terms of the social, cultural and religious ensemble in which they live and by which their thought-patterns are shaped.

But there is a further necessary step. It is the whole human race that has to be brought together in unity. The Church's ultimate function is to gather the 'nations' from the four winds into one family, one People of God, one Body of Christ and one temple of the Spirit.

> The catholicity or universality of the Church does not only mean that God's plan or his Church's mission is the salvation of all men or that the Church is to spread all over the world; it also means, and that chiefly, that the entire world as such is presented with the call to salvation and orientated towards it; that salvation is set into the very course of history; that grace penetrates the structures of the natural world; that salvation is available at the very heart of the world. By God's intervention in history, especially by God's openness to the world through the

historical event of God becoming man and rising from the dead, the whole earth has simply become a place of salvation, the world's history is simply salvation history, and time is simply a veritable moment for man's encounter with God. The intuition of Teilhard de Chardin on the Christian unity of man, of humanity and of the universe is not far from it: 'The essence of Christianity is nothing more nor less than the belief in the unification of the world, through the Incarnation. The whole history of the world is, in my eyes, one vast phenomenon of Christification.' And the universal Church is none other than mankind saved together in Christ, the sign and instrument of salvation within the creation called to salvation from the beginning. In a word, the Church as such is the bearer of and responsible for the salvation of the world as a whole.

This is not to plead for collectivism or depersonalisation, but simply to say that our care for individual salvation must be situated at the very heart of salvation for all.

For anyone engaged in the missionary task, a sense of history and a clear historical perspective are strictly necessary equipment. Some common errors in missiological method and mentality can be traced to a lack of this historical perspective. Too easily, for example, we tend to think of pagan religions as existing outside history. We often abstract them from culture and religion. We place them in a static world and a motionless history, as if they occupied some kind of cultural vacuum and religious emptiness. When we go forth with that viewpoint to evangelise a people, we feel that we must start from zero. This amounts to ignoring or destroying the values that exist already and replacing them by new imports. In this way apostolic activity becomes an act of condescension and a type of spiritual colonialism. In spite of all the good that it may do, our work becomes in fact a process of humiliation and alienation, a process of substitution instead of sublimation.

We must bring to bear on apostolic activity our own clear sense of Christian history. Christianity is not only a historical reality with a historical origin; it also has a sense and a theology of history. In the Christian view, history is rectilinear; it has a beginning, a centre and an end. God is the beginning and end of this history. He is within it, though he transcends it; he directs its course and intervenes in it. History is the unfolding and realisation in time of God's timeless plan of love and mercy for all men. God executes this plan by his interventions in human history, culminating in the death of his Son. Therefore only Christianity can view all history as a stirring narrative of divine affection and human adventure. God is the author, the master and the terminus of human history. All history is indeed a history of salvation. History is a movement with a definite purpose and in a definite direction; to accept the word of God and believe in Christ is to enter into the purpose and orientation of this movement. As a result, the Christian's attitude to the world is ever optimistic. The world is good; what is evil can be turned into good since God is present and active in the world, and since Christ has triumphed over the powers of evil.

At the same time, we must take extreme care not to be ignorant of or insensitive to the historical adventure of the people to whom we announce the gospel of salvation. For what can salvation mean if it is not inserted into the historical journey of the people to whom it comes?

> While the Christian missionary may consider it as part of his mission to inculcate a sense of history among the people to whom he is sent, he should be aware that those whom he approaches are in a given period and situation of their historical venture and have behind them, whether they are aware of it or not, a history of several thousand years.

When one asks a Chinese how old he is, he may say that he is six thousand years old! An Indian may say the same. This is not simply an expression of naïveté or a patriotic boast. It is a fact. A Chinese boy is six thousand years old. He is at the culminating point of a six-thousand-year-old Chinese culture and religious tradition.

If Christ's gospel and his Church are to transform the world, orientate history and thus lead world and history to fulfilment, they must enter into this historical movement and process.

What we say about mankind in general holds good for each country, people and nation. The missionary, whether local or foreign, must first of all enter into this history, situate himself in relation to the past and the future of its people, join in their adventure, whether it be for political independence, economic development, social reform, racial equality, cultural renaissance, up-dating of religion, cause of justice and peace or international solidarity.

Finally, a missionary must bring with him a sense of an incarnational economy, which is merely another way of saying —a spirit of genuine missionary adaptation. It is well to remind ourselves that occasional public eulogies by political leaders about our educational, medical and charitable services do not necessarily mean that the people to whom we have come regard us as being fully integrated into their country and its aspirations. This takes time, but, more important, it takes serious and conscious effort on our part to incarnate our lives and Christian message in a different people and culture.

In practice, this incarnation demands presence, purification and fulfilment. True missionary presence must be expressed in a genuine sympathy with and appreciation of the human and religious values found in other religions, and in a desire to assimilate, to our limited capacity, their ways of thinking and worshipping. This is precisely what Vatican II asks us to do: 'The Church therefore has this exhortation for her sons: prudently and lovingly, through dialogue and collaboration with the followers of other religions, and in witness of Christian faith and life, acknowledge, preserve and promote the spiritual and moral goods found among these men, as well as the values in their society and culture' (*Nostra Aetate*, art. 2).

After this, a process of purification and transformation is necessary. The Good News that we announce throws light on everything—on religious doctrines, ritual practices, and most of all on human life itself. Whenever or wherever a man meets Christ he finds himself subject to judgement. Nicodemus must have carried away much food for thought from his midnight dialogue with Christ:

> For God sent his Son into the world
> not to condemn the world,
> but so that through him the world might be saved.
> No one who believes in him will be condemned;
> but whoever refuses to believe is condemned already,
> because he has refused to believe
> in the name of God's only Son.
> On these grounds is sentence pronounced:
> that though the light has come into the world
> men have shown they prefer
> darkness to the light
> because their deeds were evil (*John* 3:17–19).

Christ is the supreme norm of existence, and every encounter with the supreme norm brings a judgement. Thus every religion is judged by the gospel, every culture is tried in the furnace of God's word. For the missionary this is a delicate and indeed a dangerous task, because it involves distinguishing truth from error and real values from false ones; to accomplish it fairly and faithfully, we must perceive these religions and cultures, as far as possible, from the inside.

Finally, there is the stage of fulfilment or consummation. Christ came 'not to abolish but to complete'; he came to lead all cultures and religions to their ultimate goal. A final quotation from Fr Amalorpavadass:

> When all the riches of the nations which were given to Christ as an inheritance (*Ps.* 2:8) are taken up by the Church in an integrated exchange, when the customs and traditions of people, their wisdom and learning, their acts and sciences are assumed and lived by the Christians, when Christians seek for understanding of the faith in the philosophy and wisdom of the new people, when their customs, and attitudes on life and social order can be reconciled with the manner of Christian living, when the ascetical and contemplative traditions of the people are integrated into the Christian religious and monastic life, when their various forms and experiences of prayer, ways of worship are integrated into the Christian liturgy, when the religious literature of other religions can be read, understood and lived with reference to the Sacred Scriptures of Christianity, then we can say that all these have been consecrated to God and thereby have reached their fulfilment and consummation in the pleroma of Christ.

Now, we have been talking at length about past errors and future ideals in our missionary enterprise. Can we suggest any method or approach for the present which reduces the risk of repeating the errors and hastens the attainment of the ideals? Here we come up against the much-abused concept of 'dialogue'. Is this really a missionary method that can help?

Those who have most enthusiastically promoted dialogue

have not always succeeded in conveying clearly its true meaning. Dialogue is not intended to be a pointless and interminable discussion at which no conclusions are reached or no ideas clarified. Similarly, dialogue does not mean a group of people searching together for what none of them either understands or possesses. Dialogue is a gentle, humane, courteous encounter in which Christians and non-Christians share their respective lights, and in which Christians show, by the use of reason and charity, that Jesus Christ is the light of the world and that he alone can bring real peace and serenity into human life.

The gospel was never intended to be a monologue. Evangelisation has not as its aim the extension of ecclesiastical influence. This would be proselytism, not evangelisation. The Church is not an end in herself; her function is to continue the work of Christ, and thus to serve people, not dominate them. Our evangelisation must always be a human meeting—of mind and heart. After all, we do not convert other people—this is not possible; we lead them to convert themselves—to turn their lives to Christ. And surely we lead them more gently and more smoothly by true human dialogue than by a condescending and imperious monologue.

Dialogue, then, is not a technique, a stratagem, a tactical weapon, a kind of cunning apostolic sheep-dog by which reluctant sheep can be rushed into the fold. We are not salesmen for some shoddy product. Dialogue is basically a frank and honest expression of an inner, deeply Christian benevolence towards other men. It is the expression of the Christian attitude of mind which enables us to listen to others rather than lecture them, to accept them rather than assess their value. It means accepting people as they are and for what they are, loving them as they are—as members of the human family and children of our loving Father. Dialogue is charity, not pity.

Perhaps we can pause here briefly to register a mild protest. Some writers on the subject of dialogue convey the impression that this is an utterly new idea, and that missionaries had better prepare themselves for a totally different approach to non-Christians. Now, it would be a vile injustice to all our missionary predecessors to suggest that they had not really loved non-Christians. Of course they had—sincerely, generously, truly. We can concede that some had perhaps loved them in spite of their non-Christianity rather than because of their humanity. But while we urge a purer motive, we do not wish to belittle past missionary virtues and achievements. Similarly, we grow tired of the complaint that missionaries in the past lived in splendid isolation from their people, turned their Christian communities into ghettoes, and kept their followers away from the mainstream of national and social life. True, we could have practised more fully the virtue of adaptation, but this does not bestow on any contemporary the poetic licence to exaggerate. Besides—somebody must say it—it is easy to counsel, theorise and dogmatise from afar. Missionaries have suffered more than their due share of bland, well-intentioned but inapplicable advice from armchair experts safely separated by thousands of miles from a mission station.

The true concept of dialogue is based mainly on a profound respect for the human person, and a greater sensitivity to each person's spiritual nature and therefore to his freedom. Respect for each man's dignity as a free human being is written into every document of Vatican II, but especially, as one would expect, into *Nostra Aetate* (Non-Christian Religions), *Ad Gentes* (Missionary Activity) and *Dignitatis Humanae* (Religious Freedom). In this last document, articles 9–11 indicate the biblical basis of this freedom of the individual and of the consequent apostolic approach. Here are some typical statements from article 11:

'God calls men to serve Him in spirit and in truth. Hence they are bound in conscience but they stand under no compulsion God has regard for the dignity of the human person whom

He Himself created; man is to be guided by his own judgement and he is to enjoy freedom.'

Christ 'refused to be a political Messiah, ruling by force; He preferred to call Himself the Son of Man, who came "to serve and to give his life as a ransom for many" (*Mark* 10:45). He showed Himself the perfect Servant of God; "a bruised reed he will not break, and a smoking wick he will not quench" (*Matt.* 12:20).'

'He bore witness to the truth, but he refused to impose the truth by force on those who spoke against it. Not by force of blows does his rule assert its claims. Rather, it is established by witnessing to the truth and by hearing the truth, and it extends its dominion by the love whereby Christ, lifted up on the cross, draws all men to himself.'

The advantages of Christian dialogue as a missionary method hardly need to be spelled out. At the first point of contact, in the pre-kerygmatic stage, it enables us to approach non-Christians on an equal level—not talking down to them, not producing a European civilisation for their admiration, not wounding their sensitivity by disparaging comparisons. It enables us, for example, to come to their assistance by all forms of Christian charity without turning these into subtle or not-so-subtle tactical inducements to conversion. Thus we can contribute to education, and medical and social work, without the suspicion of proselytism, and we can give material aid to under-developed areas without hurting people's extreme sensitivity and independence—an increasingly important consideration in both young countries and young churches.

In the work of evangelisation proper, dialogue is the most Christ-like method of making disciples. Making disciples means e ading people to follow the person of Christ—and this can never be successfully done by arm-twisting or patronage. It must be done, as Christ himself did it, by presenting the evidence, by discussing patiently, by listening to many questions and many objections, by being readily and constantly available to people: 'You see how the crowd is pressing round you' (*Mark* 5:31).

Secondly, in the present historical climate, this is the only form of evangelisation that seems to guarantee acceptance. We must be more keenly sensitive to the rights and feelings of others than we have often been in the past. This does not make our task easier; it makes it more demanding because this kind of genuine conversation with men of another language and another culture will not become possible without effort. It will demand a real knowledge of the people's way of life, their history, their stories and their way of telling them, their customs and rules of courtesy, their social conventions. It will demand a true love for them, an appreciation of their achievements as well as their difficulties, and daily, friendly, simple meetings with them in home and farm. And all this means a knowledge, no matter how painfully acquired, of their language. Without this, dialogue will remain a mystic word, floating ineffectually in the pale sky of a missionary's day-dreams.

An important element of dialogue, and one not sufficiently stressed, is its capacity to enrich immensely the missionary himself. In dialogue we receive as well as give. When we approach other peoples and other religions in this open and humble attitude we begin to see that they have much to tell us, much to give us, much to make us think. As Fr Congar has written: 'The missionary task is not merely the act of carrying light where there is only darkness; it is also a fellowship and a sharing.'

In an honest dialogue with non-Christians, every missionary is forced to re-discover himself and his own personal faith. The values he finds in other religions serve to increase his appreciation and understanding of his own gift of faith in Jesus Christ. In coming into contact with the riches and occasional heroism of other religions, he is stirred to a greater sense of the beauty and the dynamic demands of true evangelical charity. When a man admires, for example, the teaching and practice of Gandhi on non-violence, he is led to an examination of conscience on his own fidelity to the gospel's message of peace. Besides, dialogue can be a healthily humbling experience—making us more keenly aware of our own unworthiness to carry so sublime a message, and of the thirst we find in good people everywhere for the full possession of the truth and of him who is the Truth.

In this context it is instructive to read, once again and slowly, chapter 4 of John's gospel, the story of Christ's contact with the non-Jewish woman under the shade of a few trees beside a well near Sychar. Between the Jews and the Samaritans at the time of Christ there were many ancient grudges and bitter memories of former days. In such cases somebody must step forward to break the circle of suspicion, and it often takes heroic charity to do it. Most significant of all is the way Christ opens the dialogue —not by preaching to the woman, even though he is a travelling preacher by profession; not by demonstrating his control over men and nature, even though the power of God flows out from him. All this can come later. He begins the dialogue by asking for help, by asking for the only thing that this poor woman can give him—a drink of cold water. He received before he gave; he asked for help before he offered any. Our dialogue will be most effective when it begins with an act of humility.

8 Development as a Missionary Task

No discussion of present-day missionary work is complete without some mention of development and its place within the scope of the Church's apostolic activity. But in a conversation with missionaries the word 'development' is likely to provoke three quite different points of view. One reaction is sure to come, and generally from veteran missionaries who have suffered the burden and heat of the day in their efforts to build schools and hospitals. Their viewpoint normally takes the form of a rather testy question: What's so new about all this development? We have always been doing these things.

The reply is, of course, that missionaries always have striven to promote the human welfare of the people among whom they worked. It could hardly be otherwise, because missionary work is the expression of brotherly love without limitations or boundaries. Missionaries have always felt it to be part of their task to give food to those who had none. They have worked especially to give intellectual food, following the example of Saints Cyril and Methodius in Moravia, who in the ninth century invented for the Slav peoples an alphabet still in use. Schools, clinics, hospitals have always been considered just as integral and necessary a part of mission work as churches and mission houses—and often received much more attention. The statistical returns of the average mission diocese confirm all this. So we must pose the question: are all these activities—our mission schools, hospitals, etc.—really development work as it is understood today? Is 'development' merely a new label attached to a traditional missionary operation?

Another point of view is that of the missionary who, by force of circumstances and the decision of his bishop, finds his whole day taken up with works of development, and who knows by heart the names and addresses of all the important people in Misereor and Caritas. He is entitled to protest: now that so much emphasis is being placed on the preaching of the word, the carrying of the Good News, kerygma—do I really have any part in true missionary work, or have I lost my identity as a missionary behind a cloud of chalk-dust or a pile of reports for international organisations?

Thirdly, his brother-missionary whose work is exclusively pastoral may now be a little confused and disturbed by the new pressures for development. He is justified in feeling occasionally that his spiritual mission has been overtaken and swallowed up by rather secular and highly technical aid programmes, whose relation to the gospel message is not always transparently clear.

All this questioning can be reduced to two basic problems: What is development? What is the precise place of development in the ensemble of missionary activity? In attempting to answer the first we can hardly escape answering the second.

Development must be understood in the sense in which Pope Paul uses it in his 1967 Encyclical *Populorum Progressio*. It has always been found easier to say what development is not than what it is; its absence makes a more obvious and dramatic impact than its presence. Thus most descriptions of it start from negatives, and *Populorum Progressio*, article 6, is no exception: 'Freedom from misery, the great assurance of finding subsistence, health and fixed employment; an increased share of responsibility without oppression of any kind and in security from situations that do violence to their dignity as men; better education—in brief, to seek to do more, know more and have more in order to be more: that is what men aspire to now when a greater number of them are condemned to live in conditions that make this lawful desire illusory. Besides, peoples who have recently gained national independence experience the need to add to this political freedom a fitting autonomous growth, social as well as economic, in order to assure their citizens of a full human enhancement and to take their rightful place with other nations.'

From this basic description, repeated and amplified later in the encyclical, it is possible to indicate immediately some of the specific characteristics of development as the Church understands it now.

a) Like religious freedom and dialogue, it takes its origin and shape from a respect for the dignity of man. Development aims at giving every man the opportunity of living in accordance with his dignity as a free, thinking being. And the same is true of human groups: development attempts to make it possible for every nation to take its 'rightful place with other nations'. A development programme that does not stem from, and continually take account of, the human dignity of those we wish to help is not real development and, besides, stands little chance of success. 'A people quickly perceives whether those who come to help them do so with or without affection, whether they come merely to apply their techniques or to recognise in man his full value. Their message is in danger of being rejected if it is not presented in the context of brotherly love' (*Pop. Prog.*, art. 71). Frederic Ozanam said the same thing more succinctly: 'It is only because of your love that the poor will forgive you for your gifts.'

b) This respect for the dignity of others, whether individuals or nations, means that we must approach them in a particular manner. Development aid to areas and countries must be something more than a perennial donation. Its aim is improvement—and showering a man with presents does not necessarily improve him. Therefore development is not a magnanimous distribution of gifts to waiting and mostly passive recipients; it is rather the organisation of aid so that people can take an active and constructive part in building up a better future for themselves and others. This is perhaps the real newness of the idea, and it is here that we may have to make most changes in our attitude towards aid. It is in this sense that development is a modern category. It is in this sense that it differs from 'progress', which often means merely an apparent improvement in the social and economic conditions of a community, or the improvement of a limited section of a community. Development is directed chiefly to helping people improve themselves, and thus to 'those who are aiming purposefully at their complete fulfilment' (*Pop. Prog.*, art. 1). Again, material progress can be a very limited objective, and can often be prompted more by avarice than by brotherhood. And, as the encyclical says: 'Both for nations and for individual men, avarice is the most evident form of moral underdevelopment' (art. 19).

c) Development denotes the authentic improvement of the entire man. It is thus a wide and necessarily flexible term, embracing a great diversity of aspects and aspirations, and varying according to the specific needs of particular peoples and places. What is important to note here is that development does not stop short at any given point—it is addressed to the whole man, and as such must be concerned with all his needs. *Populorum Progressio* offers a wide vista: '. . . the fullness of authentic development . . . is for each and all the transition from less human conditions to those which are more human. Less human conditions: the lack of material necessities for those who are without the minimum essential for life, the normal deficiencies of those who are mutilated by selfishness. Less human conditions: oppressive social structures, whether due to the abuses of ownership or the abuses of power, to the exploitation of workers or to unjust transactions. Conditions that are more human: the passage from misery towards the possession of necessities, victory over social scourges, the growth of knowledge, the acquisition of culture. Additional conditions that are more human: increased esteem for the dignity of others, the turning towards the spirit of poverty, co-operation for the common good, the will and desire for peace. Conditions that are still more human: the acknowledgement by man of supreme values, and of God their source and their finality. Conditions that, finally and above all, are more human: faith, a gift of God accepted by the good will of man, and unity in the charity of Christ, Who calls us all to share as sons in the life of the living God, the Father of all men' (art. 20–21).

In our days, more than ever before, theology sees man as a unity—as a being of great spiritual and material possibilities rather than as a being partly soul and partly body. The ultimate aim of all development is to help men realise their full human potentialities, and therefore development must be interested in all the myriad aspects of human life in its concrete social context. It can in no way be limited to material advancement or the benefits of technology. 'Development cannot be limited to mere economic growth. In order to be authentic, it must be complete: integral, that is, it has to promote the good of every man and of the whole man' (*Pop. Prog.* art. 14). Thus, man, his health, his safety, his living conditions, his work, his poverty, his education, his family—all become legitimate objects of development. As Archbishop Helder Camara says: 'Our motto for development is the saying of Christ: "I have come that they may have life and have it to the full." ' Development, in the last analysis, is man intelligently in the service of man.

d) Besides the improvement of the entire man, development also aims at the improvement of all men. Both *Gaudium et Spes* (The Church in the Modern World) and *Populorum Progressio* express complete universality: 'And when we say man, we mean every man whatsoever and every group of men, of whatever race, and from whatever part of the world' (*Gaud. et Spes,* art. 64). 'But each man is a member of society. He is part of the whole of mankind. It is not just certain individuals, but all men who are called to this fullness of development. Civilisations are born, develop and die. But humanity is advancing along the path of history like the waves of a rising tide encroaching gradually on the shore. We have inherited from past generations, and we have benefited from the work of our contemporaries: for this reason we have obligations towards all, and we cannot refuse to interest ourselves in those who will come after us to enlarge the human family. The reality of human solidarity, which is a benefit for us, also imposes a duty' (*Pop. Prog.*, art. 17).

Development must think in terms of constituting a better world, not merely a better country. It is the building up of a true human community, a brotherhood of men. From this, two important results follow at once.

First, development in this full sense is never a purely profane exercise. This has been strongly pointed out by a Russian Orthodox layman, Nicholas Berdyaev: 'Care for the life of another, even material bodily care, is spiritual in essence. Bread for myself is a material question; bread for my neighbour is a spiritual question.' Men can live and act as brothers only when they are aware, no matter how dimly and hesitantly, of their journey together towards a common Father. And it is quite evident in our sophisticated day that as nations move closer together in terms of material progress some of them drift further apart in terms of brotherhood and charity. As technical and scientific advances enable men to come closer to each other, it is painfully clear that many men, in terms of maturity of conscience, are simply not morally equipped to cope with this new proximity. And this seems to provide an instant link between evangelisation and development.

Second, unlike aid, which can be on a small or a vast scale, at parish, provincial or national level, development is a task which demands wide planning on an international level. 'However, local and individual undertakings are no longer enough.

The present situation of the world demands concerted action based on a clear vision of all economic, social, cultural, and spiritual aspects' (*Pop. Prog.*, art. 13). Development is modern man's discovery that it is part of his function as man to harness all available human resources in order to build a more habitable world for himself and all his brothers. By definition, then, it transcends parish or even regional frontiers; it is, and must be, on the grand scale, because it has a vast programme to come to grips with. Therefore, expert and long-range planning, training in special departments or projects—these are all a necessary part of this rather typical child of the computer age. 'Individual initiative alone and the mere free play of competition could never assure successful development' (*Pop. Prog.*, art. 33).

e) Finally, and as a necessary consequence of what we have just said, a characteristic of development is that it must normally be planned and executed in conjunction with local government agencies or international fund-raising organisations. One of our duties as missionaries is to stimulate the governments of the developing countries to be more discerning in their use of their available resources; in other words, to practise self-help and self-reliance. As missionaries, we must be forever holding the plan of God before the eyes of men. And part of God's plan is that all his children should be able to live a human life on earth. This plan can be thwarted, not merely by the poverty of a country, but also by the inefficiency of a government or the avarice of a few influential politicians and industrialists. We must constantly remind the governments of developing countries of their obligations to their citizens, and stimulate them to exercise the justice and discipline necessary to fulfil these obligations. Not all developing nations are poverty-stricken; many of them have vast economic potential, but it can be tapped only by industry, ambition and honesty. An important part of our task is to awaken the conscience of civil authorities to their responsibilities in making maximum use of their resources and in sharing the resultant wealth.

Next, we must co-ordinate our own projects and assistance as perfectly as possible with the planning of the civil government. Apart from being directly in the line of development—helping countries to help themselves—this avoids a possible wasteful duplication of services. We must also stimulate the governments of the more wealthy countries to come to the aid of the developing nations. And of course the Church herself must sponsor agencies to provide money and personnel; this is a necessary form of the charity of Christ that she must show to the world of today. And the Church must be willing to supply, as far as possible, for what the local government is unable to do. However, it is wise to remember that even the most generous contributions from the whole Christian world could only scratch the surface of the world's present needs. An information paper on the United Nations agencies' plans for what they call the Second Development Decade (1970–1980) has this to say: 'According to World Bank estimates, the present yearly flow of multi- and bi-lateral aid money is about 7,000 million U.S. dollars, and the yearly flow of Church-related money 300 million. It is hoped that the yearly flow would reach in 1972 one per cent of the Gross National Product of the developed countries, approximately 12,000 million U.S. dollars, and then possibly increase to 1.5 per cent towards the end of the decade.' This gives some indication of the magnitude of the task, and also points clearly to the necessity of missionary co-operation with governments and fund-raising agencies.

So far we have made little reference to the missionary role of development. It is important to establish first of all that development aid, even if exclusively from a Church-sponsored source, must not be viewed solely as a means of evangelisation. As we mentioned above, even our best and most generous efforts are only a cup of cold water—and the cup of cold water we must, as Christians, give to our neighbour simply because Christ commands it. No further reason or motive is necessary. Thus we have an obligation to include development aid in our missionary activity and planning, independent of its ultimate practical impact on the preaching of the gospel. Obviously, as a tangible application of Christian charity, it does automatically present Christ to men, and therefore is a factor in leading men to Christ. But we must keep our motives clear. Fr Mahon, Superior General of the Mill Hill Fathers, illustrates this well in describing a visit to Molokai, the island where Fr Damien lived for nearly twenty years and died as a leper. 'Damien found an island of outcasts; he gave them a new hope and a will to live. If he were living today, he could write for help to the great national and international aid agencies; from CAFOD he would get help for his farming scheme; from Miseror he would get a hospital; OXFAM would put in a water supply, and so on . . . Damien didn't know the theory of socio-economic development or intermediate technology, but because he was a missionary he practised it. Molokai contains all the best elements of a good development project: self-help, involvement of the local people, use of local materials, "total" development: housing, education, health, religious inspiration. It is all there.'

Now to turn explicitly to the place of development in missionary activity, the following ideas were put forward by Fr Frisque in his paper of that title at the symposium.

The Second Vatican Council was convoked because good Pope John wished the Church to re-discover the true face of her eternal youth. He saw that the Church of yesterday cannot seriously and fruitfully talk with the world of today. The result of the Council's confrontation with this problem was *Lumen Gentium* and *Gaudium et Spes*. It is in them that we must search for the real meaning of development and the place it has in our mission to men.

By viewing the Church chiefly as the People of God, Vatican II acknowledged implicitly that, with the coming of the modern world, the centre of gravity of human existence had undergone a certain change in position. Formerly, man was above all a religious man, anxious to express his relation with a Supreme Being; hence his attachment to liturgy and to sacred language. But modern man is different. He is more aware of his own possibilities in the scientific and technical order; he is more independent, and often more prosperous, than his ancestors; he is a man determined to take his historical destiny into his own hands and transform the world. The language he learns and uses is secular, not sacral, and his interests tend to be in life rather than liturgy. At what point, then, can the Church establish contact with this type of man?

Beyond all doubt, evangelisation in the strict sense—presenting the Good News of salvation—is the heart of all missionary responsibility: it must be, and must continue to be. But the manner of presenting the message, and the point at which it makes contact with men—these are open to change. And, of course, our approach must be determined by the mentality and aspirations of the people among whom we work. Not all of them will correspond to the picture of 'modern man' we have just given. Most mission areas are neither industrialised nor sophisticated—and we must not import our European problems to Africa and Asia.

In simpler days, when the centre of gravity of human existence was set on the religious plane, evangelisation could only be, and needed only to be, the explicit proclamation of the mystery of Christ. In other words, it was an act expressly and exclusively religious. However, this act was always accompanied by what were called broadly 'corporal works of mercy', which had chiefly two functions: to give a pre-evangelisation form of witness which would eventually lead men to baptism and membership of the Church; to add to the proclamation of the Christian message an 'object lesson' in the charity of Christ.

If we were to retain, in today's perspective, the same attitude of mind, we should see development as an act specifically secular. For a missionary to engage in development would be an excellent thing, but distinct from evangelisation properly so called. Development and evangelisation would be two parallel but unconnected activities.

However, this viewpoint is not adequate to the new and wider vision of the Church as the People of God. We have not said everything about evangelisation when we speak of it as an explicitly religious act, nor everything about development when we describe it as an exclusively profane act. We are now in the process of discovering that man's life as such must have a religious dimension, even if this dimension is not easily or obviously or always expressed. Man's historical adventure is not an exclusively temporal enterprise. When men attempt to create a more habitable world, when they seriously strive for peace and brotherhood, they use, not merely their resources as creatures, but also and especially their essential spiritual liberty, the 'fundamental option' of their lives. Humanity's journey through history is always a dramatic paradox, because men embark on it in their condition as sinners, but at the same time the due destination and fulfilment cannot be reached unless men respond to the initiative of grace in Jesus Christ.

In this context, we can see that development is a human task with a religious dimension; Christ's unique mediation is genuinely at work there. In contributing to the development of the entire man and of all men, Christians, even though not speaking explicitly of God or faith, are still, by means of a secular language, presenting the saving word to men. In the light of the broader and more open vision of the relations between Church and world proposed by Vatican II, it is no longer possible to confine evangelisation to a specifically religious act; it is of course that, but evangelisation is also at work in all the normal forms of development, which are some of the 'essential services' that the People of God is called upon to render to the world.

Thus, evangelisation and development are not two juxtaposed activities, two parallel roads, but rather two dimensions of missionary activity, two connected levels of the unique task of the People of God. Both are necessary to help men achieve their true stature. The fundamental contribution of the Church to development is to give every man the opportunity of making, free from intolerable economic or political pressures, the basic choices which will determine his life, his destiny and his true nobility. Development of the whole man automatically includes his religious development. And that is why we find three moments in the conciliar and post-conciliar thinking on Church and world, each moving more explicitly towards a theology of development: *Lumen Gentium*, *Gaudium et Spes,* and *Populorum Progressio*. Fr Frisque understands this as a necessary and logical step in the general progress of the history of missions.

In broad terms, there have been four great eras of missionary expansion in the Church's history:

    i) the first apostolic movement—from the first to the fourth century;

    ii) the Irish monks in Europe—seventh and eight centuries;

    iii) the outward missionary movement from Europe—sixteenth and seventeenth centuries;

       the present era, which began in the middle of the last century.

Each of these eras has been shaped and determined by both the theology and the history of its own time, and this has some light to throw on our present situation.

The Acts of the Apostles reveals how joyously the first Christian communities lived their new experience of life in Christ

Jesus and how they were carried almost irresistibly to share their discovery with others. Acts 13 records the first missionary departure ceremony. Paul and Barnabas were 'sent on their mission by the Holy Spirit' (v.4), but they were also sent out by the local assembly. In other terms, the spread of their new-found knowledge and hope was regarded as a religious responsibility of the Christian community. Taking advantage of the Pax Romana and the amenities provided by the Graeco-Roman empire—highways, cities—disciples fanned out to establish Christian centres all round the Mediterranean coast. But Christians remained a minority (and mostly poor) in an empire of lofty haute culture, and they concerned themselves exclusively with the spiritual betterment of the world within the geographical limits familiar to them.

The missionary impetus of the seventh and eighth centuries was in several aspects quite different. The Irish monastic movement quickly developed characteristics that anticipated by centuries a much later general attitude: an outward-looking spirit, and a desire to combine monastic life with pastoral and educational activities. And this happened at a time when continental monasteries, more influenced by the eastern churches and their spirituality, insisted that monks remain within their cloister and withdraw from pastoral activity. The apostolic and intellectual spirit of Irish monasticism was carried to Europe by a succession of missionaries, the greatest of whom was Columbanus. They founded monasteries, not merely to be centres of cenobitic fervour, but chiefly to be nuclei of Christian life and classical learning which would radiate a spiritual and humanising influence over a wide area. From the first foundations of Columbanus, like Fontaines and Luxeuil, more than two hundred monasteries originated, a development which had a profound effect on the culture of the early Middle Ages. Evangelisation and education had proved to be a happy and fruitful combination.

By the sixteenth century the frontiers of the known world had been pushed further and further back, and the face of Europe had changed immensely. In the void following the barbarian invasions, the Church had been obliged to shoulder many new responsibilities. This led to an increasingly ecclesiastical role in temporal affairs—a mixed blessing. It meant, for one thing, that the destiny of the Church became rather closely allied to the political destiny of Europe. And, as missionaries set out from Europe to the new countries and peoples who had had no previous contact with the gospel, they went, no matter how pure their personal motives, as representatives of western Christianity, and often followed on the heels of the representatives of the European political powers. Statistically, their accomplishments were impressive, but to some 'Third World' countries even yet the missionary appears as the most insidious agent of an unwelcome western imperialism.

When the modern missionary movement surged forward in the last century it too, in many areas, worked under the aegis of a colonising power, at least to outward appearances. As in the case of the Pax Romana at the beginning of Christianity, missionaries used whatever advantages this afforded them to build up an educational network that had a giant part to play in preparing African and Asian countries for independence. But, having led these countries into the post-colonial era, the Church had to remain on there, still employing the customs and speaking the language of the departed political masters. This simple fact presented, and presents in an even sharper form today, a situation in which tact, delicacy, and much charity and patience are called for. This is where a correct application of development can build bridges.

We are the inheritors of all the missionary activity of our predecessors. We reap what they have sown, both rewards and difficulties. Thus we must both accept the historical situation of the present and interpret it in the light of past experience and future prospects; as St Bernard said: 'ante et retro oculata'. We have the opportunity of learning the appropriate lessons from past successes and failures. One of the lessons is that we can now take up a new position in regard to our young churches. As a great Anglican missionary, Canon John V. Taylor, has written: 'In the story of any new church the missionary contribution progresses through three phases: missionaries are first pioneers, then pastors, and finally partners.' The idea of partnership is admirably conveyed by our involvement in development aid. A second lesson surely is this: whatever the motives and attitudes operative at earlier stages in missionary history, now and for the foreseeable future we must be more acutely aware of the Church's real role in the history of man—the humble role of a servant. We must learn to see the Church (and ourselves as her missionaries), not as a sovereign directing human affairs in countries or continents, but as a servant of the Lord—and often a suffering one. 'And anyone who wants to be first among you must be your slave, just as the Son of Man came not to be served but to serve, and to give his life as a ransom for many' (*Matt.* 20:27–28).

Humanity is trying, more seriously than ever before, to lift itself up, to build a better future. But unaided it can only build an earthly city. By joining generously with all men, the Church as People of God can lead humanity towards a better earthly city and also to the ultimate heavenly one. This is where development comes in. St Paul worked and prayed that all things, not merely some things, would be recapitulated in Christ. When we translate this prayer into action and into the language of our time, its message is the same as that of *Populorum Progressio*: contribute to the development of the whole man and of every man. This means being at the service of men, so that they can, each in his own way, according to his own personality and history and culture, improve their lot and their lives, and enjoy a clearer vision of their true destination. Our missionary mentality, our spirit of adaptation and our apostolic activity in all its forms must take account of this.

The phrase 'a theology of development' is thrown about rather casually now, with an exasperating lack of precision and detail. Clearly, if development is to be a part of missionary activity it must have a direct bearing on the whole work of salvation and men's progress towards God. We have tried to show that the Church, in her contemporary vision of herself, sees her role as one of service to the world, and development is evidently a form of service eminently suited to both the needs and the aspirations of our age. Can we go deeper than this towards a theological and biblical basis for development work as a missionary occupation?

In a symposium paper entitled 'Towards a Theology of Development', a Dutch theologian, Fr Fiolet, approached the subject in a rather unusual way. He began by claiming that a dualist view of the universe—God in Heaven and man on earth —has given an incorrect image of evangelisation, suggesting that it is the importation of a set of immutable truths and duties labelled as gifts from heaven, even though packaged in unmistakably European language and liturgy. This dualism between the heavenly and the earthly is not biblical, but is the result of early Christianity's contact with Greek thought in aristotelian and platonic concepts. In a dualist vision of the universe anything as obviously terrestrial as development work would certainly appear foreign to evangelisation. But he goes on to argue that development is clearly seen as an integral part of the Church's message to men once we return to the Old Testament viewpoint, in which the saving action of God encompasses all worldly reality and all human history. Thus terrestrial realities form man's real meeting-place with God.

'In Israel ... men learned to know God, because they experienced his presence through concrete human situations and historical events. Very quietly, he who was still unknown caught up with humanity on the road, as with the men journeying to Emmaus. In the beginning his presence goes unnoticed, because he seems to be still entirely absorbed in their conversation. Little by little, and always in a more evident manner, he orientates the conversation (the call of Abraham), and gives it a definitive direction (the exodus). In Israel the feast of discovery takes place. Humanity recognises God in the signs which he works in its existence. Little by little, at first in a hazy and generally deformed manner, the history of man becomes the history of salvation, the history of the coming of God and of his saving dwelling within the history of man. Humanity has still a long road to travel before it discovers and can live, in the brotherly being-in-the-world of the Son of the Father, the full dimension of the saving action of God in all creation. It is by reflecting on this destiny—that is to say on the Covenant and on Christ as the accomplishment of this Covenant—that the believer grasps the meaning of his existence and the orientation of his history . . . In this prophetic interpretation of its national existence and of its history as the Covenant which Yahweh entered into with all creation, Israel acknowledged that the saving transcendental action of Yahweh is immanent in the world and is universal.'

This may be an over-simplified view of the Old Testament, because we must take account of the fact that men met God, not merely by reflection on their national history, but in the varying forms of theophany and prophecy. At the same time, this does open up a broad avenue towards further research—and it will always be true that by giving more attention to a knowledge of man we will grow in knowledge of God and his complete plan for man. However, for something approaching a theology of development, we must look further afield—and particularly to the New Testament evidence. Perhaps it is true to say that this theology will eventually be formulated by the men most intimately concerned, the missionaries themselves. As Brother Thomas More, Superior General of the Xaverian Brothers, wrote recently: 'Instead of standing before the reality with perplexity and bewilderment, religious institutes, with their sense of global dedication, ought to be in the vanguard of working out a new theology of development.'

This theology must spring from the following areas of thought: the unity of a universe created, redeemed and eschatological; Christ's attitude to material things; the young Church's understanding of this attitude.

All creation, animate and inanimate, forms a unity. Just as man is not divided within himself, so creation is not divided into man and non-man. This unity is a consequence of God's creative act, by which all things stand in a relation of dependence to him. By creation man is set over, but not over against, the world; he is told to dominate it and make it fruitful. 'God intended the earth and all that it contains for the use of every human being and people. Thus, as all men follow justice and unite in charity, created goods should abound for them on a reasonable basis' (*Gaudium et Spes*, art. 69).

This unity of creation is strengthened and sanctified by God's entry into his own created world by the incarnation. By incarnation and redemption Christ established his lordship over all creation, not merely over man. A world already directed towards God by creation is now assumed into the new order inaugurated by redemption. Not merely the dignity of man but the dignity of material things has been affected and elevated by being brought within the ambit of Christ's reign. By the unity of creation man is destined to control and thus perfect the world, for the greater glory of the Creator. But by the deeper unity of redemption, man, nature and all material things have been drawn into the divine economy of a saved world, and it is man's function and privilege to use everything in this world as stepping-stones towards the throne of the Lamb. 'Man does not live on bread alone'; he has now a new 'bread from heaven'—but this too is made of wheat.

Because of Christ's lordship, all creation awaits his second coming, when he will put the final seal of his sovereignty upon it. Therefore it is not only man but all creation that strains towards his coming and longs for fulfilment. This seems to be the meaning of Paul's mysterious phrases: 'The whole creation is eagerly waiting for God to reveal his sons ... From the beginning till now the whole creation, as we know, has been groaning in the one great act of giving birth; and not only creation but all of us ...' (*Rom.* 8:19–23). In the meantime, in the time given us before the transformation into a new heaven and a new earth, it is our task so to use and put order into the material universe and its goods that everything is directed towards the glory of its Lord and towards the hour of his final return.

The service of Christians to their fellow-men necessarily includes ministering to their material wants. In this way, material things themselves grow in dignity because they become silent witnesses to the love of Christ. In this way, too, Christ's own activity is continued in the world. It is enough to say here that his salvific activity consisted of teaching and doing —not of teaching only. Christ's life was a ministry to men, and much of this ministry was a gift of material things to satisfy physical needs of the poor and the suffering. There is no indication in the gospels that he regarded this as an insignificant activity. On the contrary, the miracles of Christ form such an integral part of his whole ministry that to remove them would distort the picture irreparably. The gospels link teaching and miracles in a perfectly consistent ensemble. Matthew, for example, places a collection of ten miracles (chs. 8–9) in between two key compilations of Christ's teaching: the Sermon on the Mount (chs. 5–7) and the 'apostolic discourse' (ch. 10). Both miracles and sermons are equally necessary to transmit the story of Christ.

Individually, Christ's miracles were acts of infinite charity and pity: 'I feel sorry for all these people' (*Mark* 8:2). But they were more than that. They were the visible public guarantees that his promises of even greater things were not empty boasts. He proclaimed himself the life of man, and began by restoring physical life to the little daughter of Jairus. He claimed to be the light of the world, and began by giving sight to the blind. He promised bread from heaven, and began by giving earthly bread to the hungry crowd.

The Church has the task of continuing Christ's ministry to men—his total ministry, the doing as well as the teaching. We cannot work miracles, but we must, more slowly and less spectacularly, attempt to feed the hungry crowds. In so doing we are obliged to use the best and most effective means at our disposal. Efficiency is a virtue. And in the present context of men's needs and resources, development aid seems to be the most effective way of bringing the resources and the needs to meet.

The importance Christ attached to charity in material things is nowhere more clearly stated than in the Last Judgement scene of Matthew 25:31–46: 'For I was hungry and you gave me food; I was thirsty and you gave me drink.' It is the criterion by which final acceptance or rejection is determined.

The early apostolic communities cherished their Master's teaching and example. The 'daily distribution' of alms to the needy (*Acts* 6) is an indication. Much has been written on Acts 4:32—'Everything they owned was held in common'—but surely *Populorum Progressio*, articles 48–49, is both a commentary on the text and an application of it to the contemporary world situation. 'We must repeat once more that the superfluous wealth of rich countries should be placed at the service of poor nations.'

From the very beginning of his missionary career Paul encouraged the local communities to share what little they had

—both as a practical act of charity and as a sign of their unity in Christ; that is how he explains the 'collection', for example, in Romans 15 and 1 Corinthians 16. St James, of course, is the great New Testament champion of the poor. What he says in chapter 2 about the Jerusalem poor of his day is still valid, both for individuals and for nations. And when applied to the present-day world, it too spells development. 'If one of the brothers or one of the sisters is in need of clothes and has not enough food to live on, and one of you says to them, "I wish you well; keep yourself warm and eat plenty", without giving them these bare necessities of life, then what good is that?' (*Jas.* 2:15–16).

Thus, the whole broad spectrum of human promotion con - tained in the concept of development is a response to the will of God and the cry of men—whether it takes the form of intellec- tual development like providing a dictionary of a local language, or the programme of the Pontifical Commission for Justice and Peace (*Pop. Prog.,* art. 5), or Credit Unions or Community Development projects. And no missionary should feel that these activities are alien to his apostolic vocation or that they reduce him to the status of a part-time missionary. However, two final points may be worth mentioning.

First, since a distinguishing mark of development is helping people to help themselves, a missionary must not attempt to do everything himself. Here is the ideal sphere in which to involve, to the maximum extent possible, the laity of both the offering and the receiving countries. This is, in fact, the sphere of the laity, because they can put their professional secular skills at the service of their brothers. Second, because respect for human dignity is fundamental to the whole concept of development there must be no trace of condescension or paternalism. The donor and the recipient must enter a development scheme as partners, and share the responsibility for its organisation and execution. From this point of view, it is important that the vastness and complexity of development planning do not make us lose sight of the real motive—the personal concern of man for man. The bureaucracy that is inevitable in such an undertaking must not seduce us from the cardinal principle that the personal touch, and personal sincerity and affection, are still the convincing proof that God loves men through men.

9 The Primacy of Proclamation

A young African priest, enthusiastically engaged in development projects in his own country, told me recently of taking part in a Study Week on Development in West Africa. At the Pax during the concelebrated Mass each day, the concelebrants, on instructions from the M.C., greeted one another, not with 'The peace of Christ' or 'Peace be with you', but with the phrase 'Progress through Development'. He was quite shocked.

We have been speaking of evangelisation and development. Now it is time to ask: can we, and should we, establish a priority between them? It is not a question of making a choice —either development or evangelisation. In this age, both must be at work together in the missionary context, the proportion varying according to the circumstances of need and opportunity. Here we use the word 'evangelisation' in its strict meaning: announcing the gospel to non-Christians with a view to faith and conversion and their eventual incorporation into the Church by baptism. Or, to use the phrase of *Ad Gentes*, article 13: announcing 'to all men with confidence and constancy the living God, and He whom He has sent for the salvation of all, Jesus Christ'. In this sense, it is not difficult to show that evangelisation has a very definite and clear primacy in missionary activity, that it is in fact the most important activity of the missionary, the central occupation around which all his work revolves.

In stressing the importance of development in the complete missionary picture, one must not be misled into believing that development is evangelisation, or is an adequate substitute for evangelisation. To say that it is an important element in missionary work is not the same as saying that it is the most important element. Even in essentials, or perhaps especially in essentials, there must be a scale of priorities. To reduce the gospel message to the solution of pressing social problems without taking any account of supernatural values could not be authentic Christianity; it would be merely a brand of what Cardinal Suenens has called 'social messianism'.

This primacy of evangelisation is not necessarily chronological; often it cannot be—it is neither Christian charity nor human psychology to start preaching to a starving man. Evangelisation enjoys pre-eminence, first because it is precisely the activity which specifies apostolic work. It is his essential orientation to evangelisation that distinguishes the missionary from all others who may work beside him: distinguishes the missionary who teaches, for example, from the lay teacher in the same school; distinguishes the missionary who spends much of his time supervising development projects from the FAO official. This is by no means an adverse judgement on the devotion, idealism or accomplishments of the teacher or the development official; it simply means that the missionary's particular speciality is evangelisation. Our work in the areas of education, medicine, development, takes its meaning and motive from the gospel, and ultimately draws its strength from liturgy and prayer.

Second, evangelisation enjoys a primacy of means, that is, it remains the chief and indispensable means for achieving the purpose of missions as defined in *Ad Gentes*, article 6: 'The specific purpose of this missionary activity is evangelisation and the planting of the Church among those people and groups where she has not yet taken root. Thus from the seed which is the Word of God, particular native churches can be adequately established and flourish the world over, endowed with their own vitality and maturity.' In the teeth of increasing and sometimes insidiously disguised secularism, it is necessary to insist that the specific task of the Church in the world is not of the temporal, social or economic order, but is of a religious nature. The gospel, and nothing else, is the leaven destined to transform, and capable of transforming, the complete life of man in the whole gamut of his relations with God, fellow-men and world.

Fr Grasso, S.J., Professor at Rome's Gregorian University, in his paper at the symposium undertook to show why the preaching of the gospel has, and must by its nature have, this primacy in missionary activity. Since it is unnecessary to go through the New Testament evidence in detail again, we will confine ourselves here to the main outlines of his thesis.

The missionary mandate in Matthew and Mark is handed down explicitly in terms of preaching: 'teach them'; 'proclaim the Good News'. It is for this reason that Christ promised to remain with his Church and with his preachers until the Parousia. Christ himself began his public life with the words: 'Repent, and believe the Good News' (*Mark* 1:15). He ended his ministry with a statement to Pilate: 'I came into the world for this: to bear witness to the truth' (*John* 18:37). There is nothing surprising in this; after all, he was the Word incarnate; his mission could only be to speak the word of his Father—to put into human speech the plan for man's salvation conceived before the world was made, called simply by Mark 'the Good News from God' (1:14).

The chief concern of the apostles in the years following the ascension was to remain faithful to their Master's mandate. They knew themselves to be 'ministers of the word' (*Luke* 1:2). When the new responsibilities of the rapidly expanding Jerusalem church crowded in upon them, they did not hesitate to affirm, by word and by practical measures, the priority of preaching—Acts 6:1-7. 'It would not be right for us to neglect the word of

God so as to give out food ... we will ... continue to devote ourselves to prayer and to the service of the word.' It is instructive to pause and notice the order of priorities here: prayer, preaching, giving out food.

Paul was so driven by his duty to proclaim the word that he feared God's eternal wrath if he did not continue to do so in season and out of season. 'Not that I do boast of preaching the gospel, since it is a duty which has been laid on me; I should be punished if I did not preach it!' (1 *Cor.* 9:16). In his great farewell speech on the sea-shore at Miletus Paul used a phrase which could well be called his autobiography: 'But life to me is not a thing to waste words on, provided that when I finish my race I have carried out the mission the Lord Jesus gave me—and that was to bear witness to the Good News of God's grace' (*Acts* 20:24).

As we have seen already, all the apostles were sharply aware of the need of organised forms of charitable activity, but they were equally aware of the priority of preaching. And for Paul, the preaching of the gospel occupied first place, not merely in his life and thought, but also among the ministries of the Church and the charismatic gifts which the holy Spirit brought to the aid of the infant communities. The question of the relative value of the various charismata had apparently become a crucial one for the Corinthian community, and Paul devoted chapters 12–14 of his first letter to the Corinthians to the problem. There he pointed out that their favourite charism, the gift of tongues, was extremely limited in its usefulness, whereas the gift of prophecy, connected directly with announcing the word, was the one they should pray for. 'The one with the gift of tongues talks for his own benefit, but the man who prophecies does so for the benefit of the community' (1 *Cor.* 14:4). Thus, in the litany of gifts given to the early Church, Paul puts prophecy, which means literally 'speaking for God', in the first place, and so above the other 'social' gifts like miracles and healing. And, ever a practical man, Paul also demands a higher temporal reward for those who preach the word: 'The elders who do their work well while they are in charge are to be given double consideration, especially those who are assiduous in preaching and teaching' (1 *Tim.* 5:17).

Does the New Testament propose any reasons for this undisputed primacy of evangelisation? St Paul's reply would seem to be based on the relationship between preaching and faith. The passage is one of the best-known of all Paul's writings.

> But they will not ask his help unless they believe in him, and they will not believe in him unless they have heard of him, and they will not hear of him unless they get a preacher, and they will never have a preacher unless one is sent, but as scripture says: The footsteps of those who bring good news is a welcome sound. Not everyone, of course, listens to the Good News. As Isaiah says: Lord, how many believed what we proclaimed? So faith comes from what is preached, and what is preached comes from the word of Christ (*Rom.* 10:14–17).

In the context, Paul is speaking specifically of the Jews, but if they cannot hear without a preacher, a fortiori the 'nations' cannot. The chain of argument is: for salvation, faith is necessary; for faith, preaching is necessary, because it is by preaching that faith in the person of Christ and his redemptive accomplishment is communicated. In this way, the primacy of evangelisation among the ministries of the Church is founded on the primacy of faith in the supernatural order. Evangelisation and faith are on the same level of importance.

This is not to deny that God, in his omnipotence and mercy, can find other ways of leading men to him, as we have seen in chapter 6. But the New Testament evidence is more than sufficient to show that the Church must expend every effort to convey the message of Christ by the only way open to her—proclaiming the word of God to men. The Church's mission is inextricably bound up with 'word'. The Belgian Fr de Rudder, who has specialised in the study of the relation between linguistic philosophy and revelation, puts forward the following ideas about preaching and the word.

In the act of speaking, man is never alone. Man builds his world and his contact with others around the use of words. Human words open up an access to others; they are the expression of a person who invites, questions and calls another to dialogue. This he does by the use of words, each of which has a content of meaning. But, besides its bare content of meaning, the human word has a creative force—seen at work, for example, in the process of imagination and of memory, and in myth. This creative power of words is found in the poet as well as in the philosopher. Everything we postulate of the human word as such is true also of word considered as the vehicle of revelation. The word of revelation carries a deep richness, because it is a revealing action which has God simultaneously as subject and object. We find its first faint cries in the prophetic word of the Old Testament experience, and its full-throated voice in the coming of Christ—the act in which the revealing word attains its supreme form and becomes a Person.

Because God has entered history by means of his Word, the word of God must resound all through history, with all its fullness of meaning and all its force and attractiveness, in the Church. And in the Church it finds expression in the dual forms of liturgy and preaching. Preaching, then, must do three things: it must express the content of Christ's revelation—the Good News of his coming and what he brought and did; it must convey to humanity the appeal that he launched—to repentance and faith; it must use human words to do all this. And it must use human words with all the creative and artistic skill of which men are capable. The privilege—and responsibility—of preaching is that it brings men face to face with the choice, the fundamental option, by which they will be either saved or rejected.

An even more profound reason for the primacy of evangelisation is that it is the operative element in the gathering together of the Christian community and thus in the expansion of the Church. The New Testament consistently sees evangelisation as a proclamation that throws down a challenge to the hearers, a challenge obliging them to take up a position towards Christ. It poses, in an official and personalised form, the old question: 'But who do you say I am?' St. Paul was infinitely consoled by the knowledge that by his preaching of the gospel men were born into Christ: 'You might have thousands of guardians in Christ, but not more than one father and it was I who begot you in Christ Jesus by preaching the Good News' (1 *Cor.* 4:15). But being born is not enough. Baptism is the beginning of the Christian life, not its consummation. Again, in an anguish almost maternal, Paul insists on the necessity of continuing to nurse the new-born Christians until they are fully disciples of Christ. 'My children! I must go through the pain of giving birth to you all over again, until Christ is formed in you' (*Gal.* 4:19). Or, as he put it another time: '. . . until we become the perfect Man, fully mature with the fullness of Christ himself' (*Eph.* 4:13). Thus, the Good News of Christ, having established the first contact with God in the missionary proclamation of the gospel, must continue to shape the lives of men. 'Let the message of Christ, in all its richness, find a home with you. Teach each other, and advise each other, in all wisdom' (*Col.* 3:16). In other words, if the Church is to grow and develop, if she is to pursue the ideal of her catholicity, it can only be by continuing to preach the gospel to every creature. The fundamental nature of the Church and of man converge on this conclusion.

To understand the primacy of evangelisation, it is both

necessary and sufficient to recall the content of the message preached. It is the unique Good News; it is the personal love story of God and men, proclaimed, proved and accomplished once for all by the God-man. No preaching will ever convey it, because no human words can ever encompass the wonder of it. The gospel has brought new life, new hope to the world. Can we isolate a single element that we can point to as the essential newness of the gospel message? Faced with this formidable question at the symposium, Fr Lyonnet, S.J., one of the greatest of Pauline scholars, gave a quite definite answer. The essential newness of the gospel lies in this: the love of man for his fellow-man is a sharing in the love by which the Father and the Son love us in the holy Spirit.

He began from Paul's description of his own mission: 'He has appointed me as a priest of Jesus Christ, and I am to carry out my priestly duty by bringing the Good News from God to the pagans, and so make them acceptable as an offering, made holy by the Holy Spirit' (*Rom.* 15:16). From that he went on to ask how Paul conceived the novelty of the Christian message, what he regarded as the specific character of the new revelation. In Paul's historical and geographical circumstances, he was obliged to define his message by reference to the Old Testament and by reference to Judaism, as he himself had known and lived it before his fateful journey to Damascus. Paul did not see the Christian revelation as a sharp rupture with the Old Testament; far from being opposed to the earlier revelation, it accomplished and perfected it. But the New Testament did, of course, surpass the Old, as all divine fulfilment surpasses its foretelling. This was a subject very much in Paul's thoughts, and he returned to it again and again, viewing it from different angles. In a *tour de force* covering the whole Pauline corpus, Fr Lyonnet indicated several lines of thought that converge on the central newness of the message that Paul carried to the gentiles.

The fundamental principle of Old Testament morality, and of Jewish morality at the time of Christ and Paul, was left absolutely unchanged by Christ's revelation; the Christian, just as the Israelite and the Jew, was by definition a man who knew how to 'please God', who walked according to the will of God. There was a 'way' of the just and a 'way' of the wicked:

> For Yahweh takes care of the way the virtuous go,
> but the way of the wicked is doomed (*Ps.* 1: 6).

The New Testament religion also is referred to as a 'way'; for example 'the Way of Truth' (2 *Pet.* 2:2). One of Paul's chief concerns for his young churches was that they would find the true way, that is, learn how to discern the will of God and have the constancy to observe it. 'That will explain why, ever since the day he told us, we have never failed to pray for you, and what we ask God is that through perfect wisdom and spiritual understanding you should reach the fullest knowledge of his will' (*Col.* 1:9).

It is precisely at this point—discovering the will of God— that we encounter the first innovation of Christianity. The Jew did not have to search for it; it was entirely determined for him by the ordinances of 'the Law'—the Decalogue and the multiplicity of precepts added to it by the temple priesthood. For the Christian, all this complex of legislation had been reduced to two commands which embraced all the others: you must love the Lord your God—and you must love your neighbour as yourself. This, however, is a relative innovation, because the Old Testament had already tended in that direction, and had stated it in so many words, for example in Leviticus 19.

At the same time, we must regard the command to 'love your neighbour . . .' as a real innovation—for three reasons.

a) Judaism tended to limit the phrase to Jews: only a Jew

was a 'neighbour'. The Leviticus formula was not helpful in this respect: 'You must not exact vengeance, nor must you bear a grudge against the children of your people. You must love your neighbour as yourself. I am Yahweh' (19:18). This explains why Christ can formulate his answer to the question: 'Who is my neighbour?' by a story, not about a pious Jew, but about a kindly Samaritan—Luke 10.

b) The Old Testament had revealed that men should love one another as God had loved them; this is said opaquely and obliquely in Deuteronomy 10. But it is clear that the Israelites had no idea of just how much God loved them. They could not be expected to have. They did not foresee that he would become man for them, that he would give his life for his sheep, in the strictest literal sense, to the last drop of his blood. Thus there is a giant difference between the practical implications of the Old Testament formula and the New Testament statement: 'This is my commandment: love one another, as I have loved you' (John 15:12). Just as the observance of the Mosaic law distinguishes the Jew from the pagan, so the practice of fraternal charity will be the unique sign by which the authentic disciple of Christ can be distinguished from all others: 'By this love you have for one another, everyone will know that you are my disciples' (John 13:35).

c) A third, and highly significant, difference between Old Testament and New in this respect is the insistence with which the love of one's neighbour as a résumé of the whole moral code is hammered home in the New Testament writings. The principle had been stated in the Old Testament; it was stated by Hillel the Elder in the rabbinic literature—but it had remained a rare and delicate flower. In the New Testament, on the other hand, we find it proposed boldly as the commonly accepted doctrine, repeated in every New Testament book. It is interesting to see that Matthew, who assembles the speeches of Christ into five large groups, brings the first one—the

Sermon on the Mount—to a conclusion with one statement of this command (*Matt.* 7:12), and concludes the final one—the Last Judgement discourse—with another (*Matt.* 25:40).

And of course in the writings of St John it becomes a refrain so frequent that, if it were less noble, would be unbearably monotonous. Likewise, St Paul's repetitions of it are too numerous to mention. It is worth pointing out that his wording allows of no possible equivocation; for example, Galatians 5:13-14: 'Serve one another, rather, in works of love, since the whole of the Law is summarised in a single command: Love your neighbour as yourself. If you go snapping at each other and tearing each other to pieces, you had better watch or you will destroy the whole community.' The same is true of the kind-hearted and blunt St James: 'Well, the right thing to do is to keep the supreme law of scripture: you must love your neighbour as yourself' (2:8).

Such unanimous insistence certainly constitutes this principle as one of the characteristics of the New Testament and therefore of Christianity. But for St Paul the real newness of Christianity goes deeper. And it is a radical newness with regard to Judaism. In spite of that, far from contradicting the Old Testament, it perfects and brings to completion what the ancient revelation had already announced.

Deuteronomy provides an apt point of departure. Chapter 10 issues a command: 'Circumcise your heart then and be obstinate no longer'—and explains it: 'It is he (Yahweh) who sees justice done for the orphan and the widow, who loves the stranger and gives him food and clothing. Love the stranger, then, for you were strangers in the land of Egypt' (v. 16; 18-19). But chapter 30 adds a vital piece of information: 'Yahweh your God will circumcise your heart and the hearts of your descendants, until you love Yahweh your God with all your heart and soul, and so have life' (v. 6). In other words, man, unaided, will not find in himself the capacity to 'love the stranger'—a thought that will give pause to any missionary. A personal intervention of Yahweh is necessary, because this is an internal renewal which God alone can effect. Interior renewal as a work of God in men is the heart of Jeremiah's great 'new covenant' prophecy in chapter 31: 'Deep within them I will plant my Law, writing it on their hearts' (v. 33).

The mainstream of Old Testament prophecy foresaw the messianic era as a great outpouring of the Spirit of Yahweh. The prophets attempted to understand and describe this in different ways, but the image used by Jeremiah—the divine handwriting on the minds of men rather than on slabs of stone—became the most popular one. It was repeated approximately twenty years later by Ezekiel (ch. 36), and echoes of it appear in Isaiah 54 and in the wisdom literature—God himself will teach men his way of salvation. They all point towards the conclusion that, in some way the Old Testament writers could not understand, the Spirit of God would become for men the interior principle of a new and higher fidelity to God and his salvific will.

This, according to Fr Lyonnet, is the essential newness of the gospel which Paul proclaimed to the pagans: 'the person of Christ, mediator of a covenant which no longer consists in the gift of a law inscribed on a stone slab and transmitted by a man, but in the gift of God's own Spirit, the mutual love of Father and Son, which Christ communicates to men by his death and resurrection, or, more precisely, by a death which, being the supreme act of love of the God-man, is the exact opposite of death and forms with the resurrection the one mystery of life.'

All this throws new light on so many startling and difficult phrases in Paul's letters. His thought was dominated, to a greater extent than we normally concede, by these two prophecies of Jeremiah 31 and Ezekiel 36. He liked to emphasise the contrast between the law written on stone and the law of the Spirit, sometimes drawing it in very sharp colours, as in

2 Corinthians 3: 'the written letters bring death, but the Spirit gives life'. Untiringly Paul repeated the same message, because he felt that it summarised the radical newness of the New Testament revelation. He used various formulae, but the doctrine remained identical. His constant meditation on the interior law of the Spirit led Paul to a point of view which found expression in terse dramatic phrases like: 'I live now not with my own life but with the life of Christ who lives in me' (*Gal.* 2:20); 'Life to me, of course, is Christ' (*Phil.* 1:21).

This too is the thought behind his words to the Colossians: 'I became the servant of the Church when God made me responsible for delivering God's message to you, the message which was a mystery hidden for generations and centuries and has now been revealed to his saints. It was God's purpose to reveal it to them and to show all the rich glory of this mystery to pagans. The mystery is Christ among you, your hope of glory' (*Col.* 1:25–27). Taking account of the whole context, this does not mean merely that the message of salvation, formerly confined to Israel, is now preached equally to the pagans, but—and so much more important—that Christ, unique source of salvation for Jews and pagans alike, has become their very life—'Christ among you'. On these verses Fr Lyonnet comments: 'I do not think that one could find a more perfect definition of evangelisation: not merely to announce Christ or preach Christ, but to plant the economy of the gospel, lead men to love one another as Christ loves us, and make them aware that this love is given to them freely by Another, Another who loved them to the point of wishing to communicate his own love by dying and rising for them and by giving himself as their nourishment in the Eucharist.'

Paul has led men a long way from the type of moralism according to which religion will simply teach them what they must do, but cannot give them the capacity to do it. His insistence on the gift of the Spirit is part of the message of hope and courage that Christianity brought to frail men surrounded by daily difficulties.

Does all this New Testament exegesis seem very far removed from our contemporary mission and its problems? The preaching of fraternal charity is always relevant, always corresponds to the needs and hopes of men. 'Missionary activity is closely bound up too with human nature itself and its aspirations. By manifesting Christ, the Church reveals to men the real truth about their condition and their total vocation. For Christ is the source and model of that renewed humanity, penetrated with brotherly love, sincerity, and a peaceful spirit, to which all aspire' (Ad Gentes, art. 8).

The world waits for the gospel. We must be willing to bring everything—bread and gospel—to the 'Third World'; we fail both God and men if we set out with bread alone. There is a lesson to be learned from the present wave of protest in the more prosperous parts of the world. A generation that has grown up in a comfortable and affluent world turns, often cynically and savagely, and rejects it, not because it has given them too much (although this is also true), but because it has given them a world without a soul. Even though they fail to express it clearly, their basic complaint seems to be that man does not live on bread alone. It is a warning that development alone—even to riches—is never enough. Men need more; they need the comfort, the support, the security of the Good News of salvation—and this only the missionary can give them. This is his privilege—and his speciality.

10 Signposts to the Future

If theology is not related to daily living, then it has ceased to be theology. And the daily living with the problems and prospects of the missionary Church is done on the missions, not at symposia or in generalates. Solutions to the current problems may be suggested anywhere, but they can be tested and evaluated only on the missions. General solutions are not particularly helpful, because situations vary immensely from country to country, not to mention from continent to continent. However, there are three broad areas of activity that will certainly have a considerable influence on the future growth of the missionary Church, and for which some opportunities exist everywhere. We can state them as:

    i) the sharing of available information;

    ii) the development of a Christian theology in local terms;

    iii) co-operation with other Christian Churches.

i) *The Sharing of Available Information*

Business circles predict that the booming industry for the remainder of the twentieth century will be the 'information industry'. Computers, information banks, the increasing facility and effectiveness of communications media—all combine to produce a torrent of information that can either aid or drown the recipient, depending on his state of preparation and his willingness to keep abreast. From the missionary point of view, the important thing is that the right kind of information flows freely to those in a position to use it in their practical pastoral work. Two items in particular are necessary information for every missionary: a) a knowledge of the social and religious customs of the people among whom he works—and much still needs to be done in this department almost everywhere; b) a knowledge of what is happening elsewhere—what experiments in adaptation are being carried out in other mission territories.

Fr Camps, O.F.M., in his paper on 'Missionary Activity and Borrowed Structures' claimed that the only way to avoid the continued importation to mission countries of non-essential and western ecclesial structures is to make both missionaries and the local churches themselves more keenly aware of the positive potentialities of the local culture, its approach to God and its forms of religious expression. And this, he said, is a task that must be undertaken by the episcopal conferences in mission countries. Only when they establish and execute a real programme of adaptation can the ideal expressed in *Ad Gentes*, article 22, be realised:

> . . . theological investigation must necessarily be stirred up in each major socio-cultural area. In this way, under the light of the tradition of the universal Church, a fresh scrutiny will be brought to bear on the deeds and words which God has made known, which have been consigned to sacred Scripture. . . . Thus it will be more clearly seen in what ways faith can seek for understanding in the philosophy and wisdom of these peoples. A better view will be gained of how their customs, outlook on life, and social order can be reconciled with the manner of living taught by divine revelation. As a result, avenues will be opened for a more profound adaptation in the whole area of Christian life. Thanks to such a procedure, every

appearance of syncretism and of false particularism can be excluded, and Christian life can be accommodated to the genius and the dispositions of each culture.

Judging by the results to date, such a programme is best carried out by the creation of a Pastoral Institute or Institute for Pastoral Research for each socio-cultural region. During the symposium discussions Fr Lyonnet recalled that he was one of several European professors invited to lecture at the Pastoral Institute of Abidjan (Institut Supérieur de Culture Religieuse), and how impressed he was by seeing African and European students, priests, religious and laity, studying together for a whole year the practical problems of pastoral activity in that very region.

Pastoral Institutes can make an immense contribution to the slow and delicate process of accommodating Christian life 'to the genius and the dispositions of each culture'. In using these words, Vatican II demands a new and deeper kind of adaptation —an adaptation not merely of a man to a situation, but an adaptation of the whole range of Christian life to different forms of expression. This call of *Ad Gentes* must not be allowed to remain a dead letter; it must be taken seriously. This is an area of activity in which we need to be more courageous than we have been; timidity is a poor substitute for prudence. To make prudent decisions, the missionaries on the spot need facts, they need information, and this demands an exchange of knowledge. Up to the present this has not been a marked feature of life in mission territories. As Fr Camps expressed it: 'We must, as soon as possible, begin research in the domain of liturgy, theology and new ecclesiastical structures. . . . The norm must be to identify ourselves, not with the tradition and history of the western Church, but with the Christian life accommodated "to the genius and the dispositions" of each civilisation. It is experimentation that will show us the path to follow, but it is also true that the experiments must develop under the direction of the episcopal conferences and the regional Pastoral Institutes.'

It might be added that experiments, no matter how successful, will be of very limited usefulness unless information about them is made available regularly and reliably. Missionaries will be denied much valuable knowledge unless episcopal conferences take pains to found, encourage and maintain magazines which will give practical information about what is happening all over the missionary world, chiefly in the spheres of liturgy, theology and pastoral practice. Only by such means can we hope to create the necessary background conditions for the full flowering of the religious and spiritual values of the local churches. And it is this alone that will make the local churches inventive and creative Christian communities, not simply pale and sometimes bewildered shadows of their European sister communities.

It is no easy task to found or maintain a bulletin of this kind in mission conditions, but episcopal conferences will have to show imagination, courage and foresight, because it is an absolute priority. This is the building up of the local church that Vatican II insisted upon so much, because theology and its liturgical expression take their origin from the life of a community. They are born of the integral Christian experience of a specific community, and they are sustained by the dynamism and energy of that community. Every missionary is willing and anxious to learn and profit from the experiences of his fellow-missionaries, and we must do nothing to hinder this. We live, for better for worse, in the age of communication, and we have a strict obligation to use the communications media at our disposal to the best possible advantage. We must gladly share our knowledge. This is a fundamental form of charity that the young churches also can offer one another—and they will all grow more vigorous as a result. Besides, this seems the only way to achieve diversity while avoiding confusion. Diversity can turn into chaos or schism or bitterness. Only deliberate and prudent effort can combine diversity with orthodoxy.

ii) *The Development of a Christian Theology in Local Terms*

At the symposium an African theologian, Mgr Tshibangu, presented a paper entitled 'The Mission and Responsibility of the Young Churches'. His chief concern was that the local churches work towards a new and native expression of the Church's deposit of revelation. He took his starting-point from chapter 3 of *Ad Gentes*: 'Particular Churches' (art. 19–22), and said: 'Having personally taken part in the meetings before the redaction of the final text as we read it in the decree, I know that a special chapter was devoted to this question in order to indicate that, at the present moment, this must be considered a matter of urgency in mission countries: to institute authentic churches, characterised by their own particularities and called to enrich the universal Church by their proper gifts and endowments.'

We have already quoted *Ad Gentes*, article 22, on the necessity of promoting theological research in 'each major socio-cultural area'. This recommendation concerns fundamental theological thinking, that is, a new examination of the data of revelation. A fortiori, a similar re-examination is called for in the areas of liturgy and ecclesiastical organisation in general. The Council issued an invitation to the young churches to bring their particular viewpoints and gifts to bear on both the institutional structure and the doctrinal progress of the Church—in other words, to give as well as to receive. In fact, the young churches in mission countries are in an ideal position to infuse a breath of new life and new thinking into our theological perspectives, because they are not trammelled by centuries-old institutions and traditions; they are relatively free to create new structures and elaborate new doctrinal formulations—to the enrichment of themselves and the whole Church. They are also relatively free from much of the turmoil and questioning which now buffet the older churches. And, as a missionary asked at one of the open discussions of the symposium, can European and American missionaries today avoid exporting some of their own confusion?

Mgr Tshibangu was particularly emphatic in claiming that the young churches have a great role, possibly a determining role, to play in theological renewal and re-thinking, even to the foundations of theological method. 'As far as Africa is concerned, for example, I am personally convinced that the African epistemological trends fall in quite naturally with the most advanced modern philosophical currents.' Several philosophers and anthropologists have noted the resemblances between the philosophic method and system of Bergson and the manner of thinking of 'primitive' peoples. As examples he mentioned: a realistic vision of the world; attachment to the concrete in intellectual processes; a philosophy of life that is basically optimistic, but neither naïve nor deceived by appearances. African ways of thought have sufficient in common with the new European epistemology to justify the hope that they can develop a theological viewpoint that will be positive, contemporary, and a valuable addition to all the ecclesiastical research and re-appraisal going on in the universal Church at present.

Mgr Tshibangu concluded by saying that the young churches should set themselves to thinking seriously about this, especially in spheres of thought where they have the greatest opportunity of adding to the Church's theological understanding. Such spheres would certainly include: man's way of viewing God, and man's expression of this in religious rites and practices; the relationship between the natural and the supernatural; the nature of sacrament; the essence of the Church, as an institution founded by Christ and as a response by men; the possibility of a re-statement of revealed truths in the context and language of a different culture and milieu—a 'demythologising' process on a local and practical level.

iii) *Co-operation with other Christian Churches*

Co-operation in missionary endeavour is handed its greatest test and greatest opportunity in the ecumenical movement. The absence of a specific treatment of this subject was a lacuna in the symposium programme. Much more serious, the slow pace of ecumenism on the missions is disturbing. All the more so because it is nowhere more necessary, since there the scandal of a splintered Christendom poses a daily question-mark for all believers.   It must be admitted that we seem to have no reliable information on how much damage it has done, or how keenly our new Christians are affected by it. And surely this is an important area of research, and a ready-made opportunity for ecumenical study. But certainly the multiplicity of Christian Churches, pulpits and preachers must sow the seeds of some kind of religious indifferentism, from which the only harvest that can be reaped is one of confusion and cynicism. And it is unfortunately true that we have been one of the most distrustful and hesitant of all the Christian bodies. As far back as 1910 the World Missionary Conference at Edinburgh brought together a number of Protestant missionary societies and Churches, and began preparing an ecumenical approach to missionary activity. We can hardly claim that our tardiness in ecumenical initiatives is due to lack of encouragement. In 1964 Vatican II said this: 'Concern for restoring unity pertains to the whole Church, faithful and clergy alike. It extends to everyone according to the potential of each, whether it be exercised in daily Christian living or in theological and historical studies. This very concern already reveals to some extent the bond of brotherhood existing among all Christians, and it leads toward

that full and perfect unity which God lovingly desires. . . .
We must come to understand the outlook of our separated
brethren. Study is absolutely required for this, and should be
pursued with fidelity to truth and in a spirit of good will'
(*Unitatis Redintegratio*, art. 5 and 9).

What ecumenism is and what it must do was spelled out in
detail by this same Decree on Ecumenism: 'The "ecumenical
movement" means those activities and enterprises which,
according to various needs of the Church and opportune
occasions, are started and organised for the fostering of unity
among Christians. These are: first, every effort to eliminate
words, judgements, and actions which do not respond to the
condition of separated brethren with truth and fairness and so
make mutual relations between them more difficult; then,
"dialogue" between competent experts from different Churches
and Communities. In their meetings, which are organised in a
religious spirit, each explains the teaching of his Communion
in greater depth and brings out clearly its distinctive features.
Through such dialogue, everyone gains a truer knowledge and
more just appreciation of the teaching and religious life of
both Communions. In addition, these Communions co-
operate more closely in whatever projects a Christian conscience
demands for the common good. They also come together for
common prayer, where this is permitted. Finally, all are led to
examine their own faithfulness to Christ's will for the Church
and, wherever necessary, undertake with vigour the task of
renewal and reform' (*Unit. Red.*, art. 4).

Some obvious conclusions flow immediately from this.
First, ecumenism is not just a passive and semi-reluctant coming
together; it is an active and deliberate working together
towards a real and visible unity of the Church. Second, the
ecumenical movement is not merely the replacement of
hostility by a correct politeness; it is a real effort to translate
John's gospel into practical living. Finally, ecumenism is not

confined to either wishful solitary thinking or social tea-parties; it is essentially a religious activity with Christ as its motive and impulse. This is what Fr Hastings means by his distinction between a 'pre-ecumenical phase' and a 'real expression of ecumenism'. '. . . ecumenical activity strictly so-called is aimed at bringing Christian disunity to an end, while the purpose of pre-ecumenism is to replace attitudes of social hostility between the denominations by a good-neighbour attitude and co-operation on the social level.'

Ecumenism, then, is not a sentimental heart-throb, but a theologically-based Christian imperative. *Unitatis Redintegratio*, articles 2–3, proposes a line of thought that could be called a theology of ecumenism. Basically, the reasons for ecumenism are: humanity is one; God's salvific will is for all; the Church Christ founded is one; his mission to the world was a mission of individual renewal and universal reconciliation; and his final prayer is given by St John as: 'May they all be one. Father, may they be one in us, as you are in me and I am in you, so that the world may believe that it was you who sent me' (*John* 17:21). It is not surprising that the word 'one' sprinkles the New Testament text: one saviour, one faith, one baptism, one body, one Spirit, one hope, one in Christ Jesus, one mediator, one covenant, one sacrifice, one high priest, one name by which we must be saved . . .

Unity is not a propaganda expedient, not an emotional appeal; it is a profoundly intimate part of God's plan of salvation. All who profess to be followers of Christ must accept his unique lordship over all men and witness to it. Each Christian worthy of the name is a witness to the Good News of Christ's coming, his raising up and his return. Thus, the witness of Christians to their Master's will and their Master's work should be one unanimous witness. But the course of human life does not run smoothly, and the Church was still only an infant when the first difficulties arose. Paul encountered them at Corinth and in Galatia. 'I am astonished at the promptness with which you have turned away from the one who called you and have decided to follow a different version of the Good News' (*Gal.* 1:6). It is only to be expected, then, that in the course of her pilgrimage through history the Church should encounter many divisions and internal disagreements. This is part of the price to be paid for the liberty of the human spirit.

It has led inevitably to the present situation, where several Christian Churches and communities proclaim the one gospel of Christ but present it to the same group of people in different ways and with different liturgies. Obviously, this clouds the original message and does not project the image of Christianity that Christ willed. For example, it is quite common to find an African town with four or five different Christian denominations, each with its own compound, church building and at least primary school. I have often been saddened on Sunday morning in West Africa to see several rival congregations moving towards their respective churches, because a potentially healthy and united Christian community was being torn apart by our imported differences. Even if we use different schools, surely we could teach religion by means of a common Bible. And how much good could be done, and how much good-will generated, by the use in all of them of an ecumenical text-book of history, particularly for the Reformation period! The writing of such a book would hardly be more difficult than a common Bible translation, and the success in this latter sphere surely gives grounds for hope.

Since all Christian missionaries go out to give witness to Christ, it is a deep and sad contradiction that we should offer competing testimonies. If we cannot yet give absolutely identical witness, at least our missionary efforts will be closer to the divine ideal and intention if we unite to give common witness. Common witness simply means collaboration between individual Christians of differing denominations as well as collaboration between differing Christian Churches to manifest the faith and the charity that are in them.

In order to discover the areas in which this combined action can be practical and fruitful, it is well to establish first a kind of balance sheet of agreements and differences. And it will emerge at once that the agreements are both more numerous and more profound than the differences. All the Christian Churches wish to proclaim the same Good News of salvation through Jesus Christ. They all accept the basic outline of the salvation story in Old Testament and New. Most of them recognise the sacramental economy established by Christ, in particular the necessity and efficacy of baptism and Eucharist. Many express their faith by means of the two great Christian creeds, the Apostles' Creed and the Nicene Creed.

This being the case, then, why cannot we unite in presenting our common patrimony of truth? The differences appear as soon as we start applying this in concrete situations, and they appear mainly in the area of ecclesiology. Each Church has built up, over the centuries, its own traditions, methods and ministries, and is unwilling to renounce them. Particularly sensitive is the question of the precise position of each Church in the context of the one Church founded by Christ.

As long as the Churches continue to watch one another with suspicion, and to speak in claims and counter-claims, little progress can be made. But if they would turn their gaze from one another to the world, and look out on the millions of men who are totally ignorant of Christ's message, then perhaps all Churches would become aware of their common obligation to carry the news of Christ's redemption by the most effective means possible. And it would be helpful to all of us if we would regard missionary zeal, not so much as a quest for clients, but as an exercise of Christ's charity to which we are all equally obliged. And this outward-bound charity will enable us to separate the essential kernel of the Christian message from the formulae in which it has been traditionally presented and the non-essential additions that have grown up around it.

Vatican II has warned us to be quick to read 'the signs of the times' and seize the graces of the moment. The truths of faith we cherish—these we must continue to cherish and to preach; that is not in question. But it may be useful to remember that many of these truths have been formulated in stormy eras of upheaval and opposition; this did not alter the truth, but it did determine the doctrinal formulation of it. Now the times are, from some points of view at least, less stormy, and there is a welcome atmosphere of good-will, a conscious desire on the part of all Christians to unite. We must avail of this atmosphere to search for ways of proclaiming together our common deposit of truth, and to seek contemporary expressions of it that will savour of common witness rather than controversy, of service to a needy world rather than closed-circuit polemics. And this provides a vast field of research 'already white, ready for harvest'.

There are several steps we can and must take at once. In most mission countries the opportunities for ecumenical action are certainly not lacking. And such action is to the advantage of all —that of the whole Church and that of the people the Church wishes to serve. All the Churches are face-to-face with the same difficulties, the same challenges, the same opportunities. It does not make sense to meet them any way except together. The arguments in favour of joint action, of common witness, are infinitely stronger than those brought forward against it, which often, on closer view, turn out to be an ingenuous amalgam of fear, conservatism and laziness. Thus there seems no valid reason for further delay or hesitation. There are many furrows to plough.

In 1968, Dr Visser 't Hooft, addressing an Assembly of the World Council of Churches, said: 'It must become clear that Church members who deny in fact their responsibility for the needy in any part of the world are just as much guilty of heresy as those who deny this or that article of the faith.' The whole area of development presents an obvious opportunity for common witness. A significant step in this direction is the establishment of such an organisation as SODEPAX—a Committee for Society, Development and Peace co-sponsored by the Holy See and the World Council of Churches. The programme of this Committee is to establish, at all ecclesiastical levels, inter-denominational groups to discover the factual situation, and then elaborate a joint policy by which the entire Christian commonwealth can proceed to work towards genuine world justice. A part of this gigantic programme is the evaluation and co-ordination of aid stemming from the Churches, and the integration of this aid into the national development planning of particular governments. We must learn, and quickly, to work with rather than in competition with all men of good-will.

Most business organisations have long since learned the value of common planning—in fact, its necessity for survival. We must be more generous in sharing our knowledge, much of it so patiently and painfully acquired. There is so much valuable help we can give each other in facing practical and pressing problems like those of Christian witness in colleges and universities, the Christian renewal of the family, the general struggle against increasing social ills—illiteracy, poor housing, prostitution, the rush to the cities. As Fr Stransky, of the Secretariat for Promoting Christian Unity, asks: 'Can any one Church in Africa muster enough talent within its own ranks even to *study* properly the urbanisation problems: the novelty of most urban employment, the moral challenge of the anonymity of the individual in the crowd; the housing problem and the high rent and congestion that follow, the loss of privacy, and the breakdown of the clan into single-cell families? What old structures in the parochial life of all the urban Churches—

good though they may have been, good though they still must be—must die precisely to stress both the financial and man-power priorities in the new situation?'

It must surely be taken for granted that we should, in sheer justice to our common Christian heritage, preach and pray together. Even now, in our incipient ecumenism, we have so much in common to proclaim to a Christ-starved world, and so many things to pray for. But our proclamation and our prayer will gain immeasurably in breadth and profundity from some common theological research. The mysteries of God, of faith, of salvation, will always be too great for human thoughts and therefore for human words, but we can clear away much unnecessary confusion and misunderstanding by studying these mysteries together rather than in some kind of slightly sus-picious opposition, or in lonely and proud isolation.

Closely allied to this is the vital area of a common study of religions and cultures. We need this knowledge urgently, and we can obviously obtain it more easily and more rapidly by combining forces in a concerted study than by individual and sometimes myopic efforts. It is scarcely necessary to prove that the pooling of all our Christian resources of manpower, imagin-ative thinking and constructive suggestions is the only reason-able procedure, and the only one likely to provide solutions to the problems we face. Let's take as an example a tiny segment of this question of the study of religions. In recent years the phenomenon of native, independent African Churches has become increasingly evident—and is a source of both interest and anxiety to missionaries. At present there are over 5,000 such Churches in sub-Saharan Africa alone, some with exotic names and equally exotic rites, but all of them schisms from the traditional Christian Churches. While most are statistically insignificant, together they number about eight million mem-bers. Up to a few years ago missionaries were inclined to dismiss these Churches rather contemptuously as a schismatic reaction to foreign missionaries and an imported religion. But is this the complete explanation? We are far less certain now. From a closer study it seems that in most cases the chief motive was a deep desire to create a community that could express its Christian faith in a truly African manner. Their success and their sureness of vision vary immensely, but their aims are often admirable; for example, the Zambian 'Catholic Church of the Sacred Heart' was founded to give a specifically African expression to the Franciscan ideals of poverty and preaching.

The growth of these Churches—often much more rapid than our growth—merits serious study and investigation. It poses a sharp challenge to all Christian Churches to examine their own methods and principles of adaptation, and to learn how far removed our staid western liturgy and theology can be from the vibrant African spirit. This could lead to some important developments in our preaching, our eucharistic celebration, and our administration of sacraments. Again, we can make no progress without a free flow of information; for example, how many missionaries in Africa are aware of what the Dominican Fathers are doing in Malumfashi (Nigeria)—attempting to train African catechists for an African Church; or of what the Maryknoll Missionaries are doing in Musoma (Tanzania)—attempting to develop African communities which are truly Catholic while being also truly African?

Finally, but perhaps most important of all, we have much to learn from existing ecumenical initiatives concerning the Bible. To quote Fr Stransky again: 'If, in history, it has been the word of men that has divided us, it will be the word of God that will draw us together.' Ecumenical Bible work is an experience of particular interest to both mission and non-mission countries, first because it is already under way and achieving results, and also because it shows what can be accomplished, even in an extremely sensitive area, by honesty and perseverance. It may be worth while to review rapidly how work towards a common

Bible was planned, the human and theological difficulties that were encountered, and the methods by which they were surmounted.

The possibility of a common translation of the Bible by and for all Christians really arose from the meeting of two independent currents in the Catholic Church in the decades preceding Vatican II: the biblical movement and the ecumenical movement. The two were brought together by a happy combination of circumstances connected with the Council. *Dei Verbum*, the Constitution on Revelation, sent bishops, priests and people back to their Bibles in no uncertain manner. The instructions were clear, the language unequivocal. 'But since the word of God should be available at all times, the Church with maternal concern sees to it that suitable and correct translations are made into different languages, especially from the original texts of the sacred books. And if, given the opportunity and the approval of Church authority, these translations are produced in co-operation with the separated brethren as well, all Christians will be able to use them' (*Dei Verbum*, art. 22).

But even before that, Vatican II had urged the restoration of the liturgy in the vernacular, in the first document it issued — *Sacrosanctum Concilium* (Constitution on the Liturgy). Since so much of our liturgy consists in scriptural readings, bishops in mission countries suddenly found themselves with a new problem; particularly in Asia and Africa there were no Bibles in the local language. However, in most places there was a translation of the Bible made and distributed by the Bible Societies. The United Bible Societies is a union of 35 national Bible Societies, at present operating in over 150 countries, which has long been at the service of Protestant Churches in publishing cheap vernacular Bibles.

Soon after the promulgation of the Constitution on the Liturgy in 1963, bishops and priests in mission countries began writing to the Bible Societies for permission to use their Bibles, or to inquire if the Societies could produce new translations. The language problems of mission countries can be enormous. Since statistics can be simultaneously imposing and bewildering, perhaps we can give a clearer picture by taking one country, Nigeria, as an example. In Nigeria approximately 250 languages are spoken. In preaching and catechesis, missionaries use English, Yoruba, Ibo, Hausa, Idoma, Efik, Gwari, Edo, Tiv, Ijaw, Urhobo and Igala. A translation of the gospels is available in all these languages, but the complete Catholic Bible is available only in English. And missionaries in Nigeria are agreed that all the translations need to be re-worked. Partly for these reasons, and partly because it came into being during the Vatican Council, the Bible Society of Nigeria was the first in the world to have Catholic membership at all levels right from the beginning.

Encouraged by the new ecumenical spirit with which the Council was being conducted, the United Bible Societies wrote to the late Cardinal Bea, President of the newly-created Secretariat for the Promotion of Christian Unity, asking if there could be discussions of common policy about translation and distribution of Bibles throughout the world. Cardinal Bea readily agreed that a group should begin work on a tentative draft of general guiding principles for a common translation. The group began work in November 1964 at Crêt Bérard, Switzerland, and this work concluded in 1967 with a meeting in Rome between Cardinal Bea and Dr Holmgren, Chairman of the United Bible Societies, and a group of experts, at which a document outlining guiding principles for translation was given final shape.

This document was published simultaneously in Rome and London in June 1968 under the title: 'Guiding Principles for Interconfessional Co-operation in Translating the Bible.' It is a fascinating text, and highly instructive as a plan of campaign for all kinds of ecumenical co-operation, because of its attention to detail, its charity and spirit of mutual give-and-take, and its realistic acceptance of, and approach to, the human problems of ecumenism.

For example, the question of the Old Testament Canon could have proved a major stumbling-block, since most of the Churches regard the seven deutero-canonical books, and sections of seven other books, as apocryphal. However, in recent years the Bible Societies have acted on the principle that it is the Churches themselves, not the Bible Societies, that must determine the Canon of Scripture. So they agreed to apply this principle to the Catholic Church also. Thus the text says: 'It is recognised that on the one hand an edition of the complete Bible bearing the imprimatur of the Roman Catholic authorities will contain the deutero-canonical texts and that, upon the other hand, while many groups within Protestantism have employed the Apocrypha, a great majority find it impossible to accept an arrangement of the Old Testament which does not clearly distinguish between these texts and the traditional Hebrew canon. It is suggested that these two positions can in practice be reconciled if normally, in editions of the Bible published by the Bible Societies and bearing the imprimatur of the Roman Catholic authorities, the deutero-canonical texts are included as a separate section before the New Testament.'

Another serious hurdle was the question of notes added to the scriptural text. Canon 1391 legislates that Catholic editions of the Bible have annotations. On the other hand, the Bible Societies have always published their Bibles 'without note or comment'. Both sides finally agreed to meet halfway. The Bible Societies' prohibition is limited to dogmatic and interpretative notes, so that they are willing to employ annotations that give historical background information, explanations of proper names, etc.

Strong clashes of opinion can arise even in such a restricted area as the spelling of proper names. This is immediately obvious in English translations, where centuries of usage have accustomed people to a 'Protestant' spelling (Jeremiah) and a 'Catholic' spelling (Jeremias). The document says that each group of translators must reach agreement on this point before they begin work, and suggests as a basic principle that the names should be as close as possible to the original Hebrew or Greek forms, adding however that 'certain widely known forms of names may be so deeply embedded in popular or local usage that they cannot be readily changed'.

In an admirably practical section entitled 'Procedures', the document indicates a general course of action for a co-operative venture in Bible translation. Starting from the principle that 'it is preferable to undertake a new translation rather than attempt a revision of an existing text', the statement suggests the composition of three groups: a working committee of not more than six people who have both the knowledge and the time necessary to undertake the translation work; a review committee of experts; and a group of 'consultants', representative of both the Churches and the areas being catered for by that particular translation.

Putting past experience to use, the document insists that somebody be appointed to take the ultimate responsibility for editorial supervision. It gives a sound, down-to-earth reason: 'Such supervision, however, does not necessarily entail constant "watching" of the work, but rather provides a means by which the translators may have from a competent Bible Society source some guidance as to ways of solving those problems which may have arisen during the course of the work. Moreover, the possibility of such consultation provides a method for eliminating pressures which may build up when there is no such "neutral referee" to which to turn. The mere fact that such consultation is available ... often prevents tensions and the development of strained relations.'

At present, joint translation projects are well under way in many parts of the world. The best known is probably the French 'Ecumenical Translation of the Bible', which courageously began with the epistle to the Romans, a notorious theological battlefield. Their translation of the epistle to the Romans was published in 1967, and several other volumes have followed since. This translation of the Psalms is being used in the new French text of the Breviary.

Enough progress has already been made to prove, even to the pessimistic, that ecumenism is not an impossible ideal. Besides, so much prayer and work for unity will certainly not remain unrewarded and unproductive. And it is chastening to recall that, in earlier days, there have been splendid examples, now mostly forgotten, of good relations and high principles in matters ecumenical. The Chairman of the United Bible Societies Executive Committee, Dr Holmgren, courteously recalled this at his meeting with Cardinal Bea in January 1967: 'It was at the very outset of the Bible Society movement, more than one hundred and fifty years ago, that initial friendly contacts were made between the groups represented here today. The British and Foreign Bible Society in London was from the beginning in frequent communication with Roman Catholic leaders and at a very early stage had sanctioned and circulated as many as eight Roman Catholic translations of the Scriptures in the principal languages of Europe. Similarly, Roman Catholic churchmen were invited to participate in the formation of the American Bible Society a few years later. However, the bright promise of those early days was eclipsed by a long period of mutual misunderstanding and mistrust, an eclipse that has now, praise God, given way to a bright new dawn.'

Every missionary today could fruitfully meditate a little on a paragraph in Fr Hastings' book, *Church and Mission in Modern Africa*: 'It is good to remember that the Catholic proto-martyr of modern Africa, St Joseph Mukasa Balikuddembe, was killed in 1885 because he had bravely spoken up against the murder of the Protestant Bishop Hannington; that the last night the body of David Livingstone spent in Africa was in a Catholic chapel, of the Holy Ghost Fathers in Bagamoyo; that it was a Protestant minister who presided over the funeral and prayed at the grave of Bishop de Marion Bresillac in Freetown in 1859. Best of all, our martyrs died together. Catholic and non-Catholic were burnt side by side at Namugongo for their common belief in Christ, the Protestant Alexander Kadoko as well as his uncle the Catholic Bruno Sserunkuma. It seems sad that in canonisation they should be divided. We have indeed always shared a common brotherhood, but brothers must come together around the same table and go out from it to work in harmony.

11 The Missionary Mentality

'Fundamentally the Mission is not man's action but God's; it is
for the Christian to choose whether he will be caught up into
it and participate in it, or remain outside. It is proclamation but
never propaganda, for propaganda smacks too much of human
stratagem. It is not proselytising, for God does not prosely-
tise; He calls and waits and judges; He seeks and serves and
suffers.'

These words of Canon Taylor, Secretary of the Anglican
Church Missionary Society, sum up much of what we have
been trying to say. Most missionaries, too, have experienced
what it is to seek and serve and suffer. This they did, generally
without demur, until our contemporary era of universal
interrogation began to ask them what they were doing—and
why. And some did not hesitate to pose the question in biblical
form: 'Why this waste?', conveniently forgetting that St John
attributed this question to Judas. However, for his own peace
of mind and clarity of vision, every missionary needs clear
unequivocal answers to three fundamental questions—and he
needs these now. Whose representative is he: of the eternal
Christ, 'the same today as he was yesterday and as he will be for
ever' (*Heb.* 13:8), or of a possibly out-dated missionary
institute? Is his daily apostolic activity really what he should be
doing, is it what Christ asked for—or is it merely a fading echo
of ancestral ideals? Finally, is there a continuing compelling
motive which will sustain him in tolerating all disappointments
and in devoting his life and energy to the task of evangelisation?

This chapter is simply a rag-bag of random remarks that hinge around these three questions.

We have attempted, in the early chapters, to give the real reasons for missionary activity. They are to be found in Scripture and in the current theological understanding of the Church and her mission. The Old Testament pointed un-erringly towards a missionary movement that would suffer no geographical or historical limitations, that would be to all the nations. The gospels acknowledge the same universality, and add the explicit and even peremptory command to go and make disciples of all the nations. The Acts of the Apostles and the New Testament epistles reveal missionary endeavour in action and provide a kind of 'visual aid' to its component parts: dedicated apostles, an expanding Church, local communities enthusiastically living a new life in Christ.

Theologically, the Church's increasing understanding of herself is now expressed in terms of the People of God, the pilgrim Church, and the Church as essentially and intrinsically missionary. An important element is that the mission of the Church is anchored radically in the Trinity—in the family nature of God and in the divine sending forth of the Son and of the Spirit. This means that the Trinity provides the ultimate motive for missions. Our task as missionaries is to lead men to the Father, and 'no one knows the Father except the Son and those to whom the Son chooses to reveal him'. Further, no one comes to the Father except by becoming his son. Mission-ary activity is our attempt to translate the mystery of man's creation into the greater mystery of man's adoptive sonship.

After all, we are simply trying to lead men to their true destiny—their destiny as sons of God. We are trying to tell them and show them that, in order to be fully men, they must know themselves to be fully sons of their Father. And this they can become only by means of the perfect Sonship of Christ. But, as Paul points out, men can turn to God and say 'Abba,

Father' only by the power and the light of the Spirit. 'Everyone moved by the Spirit is a son of God. The spirit you received is not the spirit of slaves bringing fear into your lives again; it is the spirit of sons, and it makes us cry out, "Abba, Father!" The Spirit himself and our spirit bear united witness that we are children of God' (*Rom.* 8:14-16).

We do not know the workings of God's Spirit or how he leads men to a knowledge of their sonship. But a reading of John and Paul leaves us with the conviction that it is only the holy Spirit who can give the saving faith in Christ that is the key to sonship and salvation. We can tell a man the story of his salvation, but only the holy Spirit can bring that message to life in his heart. And, of course, only the holy Spirit can give us the humility, the simplicity and the charity to tell our story as it should be told. Only the holy Spirit will give us the courage to continue proclaiming the love of Father and Son in spite of opposition, frustrations and apparent fruitlessness, in spite of the indifference of the unconcerned and the cynicism of the unconvinced. And when the holy Spirit presents us with unexpected opportunities—and every missionary has experienced them— we must not hesitate to grasp them. As Bishop Newbigin has written: 'Faithfulness to the New Testament must bring us to give to the Spirit a much more central place, not merely in the theory but also in the practice of Missions. He is still sovereign and free—free to do the unexpected thing that astonishes us, just as Peter and the Elders at Jerusalem were astonished when his manifest presence was given to the uncircumcised Gentiles. He opens up ways that the missionary never expected, and when he does so the missionary must follow. He chooses as his instruments people who would never have been selected by the missionary, and when this happens his decision must be honoured.'

The ways of God are far outside the ken of man, and the mystery of salvation is exactly that—a mystery. Every man carries within him the stamp of his divine origin—and deep calls to deep in ways beyond our knowing. One of our great unanswered questions is that of the salvation of men outside the reach and range of the Church founded by Christ. We can only accept facts, and trust in the Lord of the world to establish his contacts with the world in any of the infinite variety of ways his eternal wisdom determines. In this we are merely spectators, but we should be grateful to be even spectators at the continuous and unmerited outpouring of God's love. This should not be regarded as an obstacle to our missionary activity, but rather as a greater impetus. What sportsman wants to remain merely an impotent spectator when he can play a part in the victory of divine goodness over human frailty and error?

Again, we have looked at this question from the viewpoint of respect for the dignity of the human spirit. Man is a free being, with all the possibilities and all the responsibilities that this entails. And respect for his freedom must determine our apostolic approach to him. We come to meet him—person to person—and unless this is done with mutual trust and respect, there is either domination or artificiality. Neither finds a place in the Christian catalogue of virtues, and neither is an apostolic charisma. This profound, genuine, unforced respect for the human person is operative in all missionary work, but has particular reference to the areas of dialogue and development. We must ask ourselves bluntly: are we, or are we not, willing to meet every man as an equal, and, for example, to take our new Christians into our full confidence? How disinterested are we? Or more positively, how genuinely interested are we in the good of individual men and the welfare of the communities they live in, their cities, their countries? How sensitive are we to the needs, the feelings, the ambitions, the aspirations, as well as the inevitable eccentricities, of other peoples?

The fields of dialogue and development are sufficient to test the skills and the personality of any missionary. There are no rule-of-thumb standards here. Our approach, and the extent of our involvement, must be judged on the spot in the light of the actual conditions of men and means. There are two sides to every coin, and we must remain aware of both. For instance, we have devoted a chapter to the importance of development, and followed this by a chapter on the priority of evangelisation. Does this seem a contradiction? In fact, it is not, but it does underline the need to balance our activities—to see both sides of the coin. The correct balance cannot be indicated in any text-book, because it will depend exclusively on the local situation in which the missionary finds himself. The degree and kind of development to be aimed at must also be decided on the spot, and must keep pace with the changing social, economic and political movements in the particular region. In one country our energies may have to be directed to procuring aid from outside, in another to spurring the local government into being serious about its responsibilities to its people. And this latter task is generally the more difficult of the two—requiring more patience, more courage and more tactful handling.

Again, the degree and kind of dialogue that the missionary is called upon to exercise will vary according to the stage at which his young community finds itself. As a parish grows in numbers the missionary's tasks increase, and many of his contacts with the people will necessarily be through the medium of others, like catechists and teachers. The missionary now has the more delicate task of transferring his own attitude and his skill in dialogue to them, so that their contacts with non-Christians will be of the right quality. It is really only then that a tightly-knit and vigorous Christian community can come into being, because only then are the local Christians themselves involved in the building-up of the community, and a particular young church is learning to be itself mission-minded. To achieve this, the missionary must delegate some of his traditional authority to individuals or groups in the community. This is more, and

more important, than merely a step towards 'laicisation'. It is
that, of course, and as such is a necessary step. But basically it is
the creation of an atmosphere in which a young church learns
to use its own resources, to bestir itself, to make efforts for itself,
to cease relying for direction, instructions, permissions and
finance on the 'foreign' missionary. We have founded many
institutions—colleges, hospitals—that would not have been
founded otherwise. Perhaps we are entitled to feel a certain
pride in them, but we certainly are not entitled to feel possessive
about them. And it is much better now that the day-to-day
running of them be organised by lay committees, parents
associations, etc. This may not, to our minds, produce the most
efficient results, but it does help an infant church to begin
walking unaided. And this is an aim towards which we strive.

There are several sectors of the normal administration of a
parish that can be dealt with by parish committees. Handing
responsibility over to them will not, initially at least, make the
missionary's life easier—but that is not a weighty argument
against it. And we must give these organisations a reasonable,
sensible autonomy; this is an essential part of our exercise of
dialogue with them, and is a necessary beginning if they, in their
turn, are to grasp and maintain the spirit of dialogue. Fr Hastings
aptly remarks: 'If it is the Gospel not the Law that we are sent
to preach, it is a life of freedom not of compulsion that we must
build up. Almost everywhere in the past the Church has tended
to be over-authoritarian, but this is particularly true in the
missions.'

Still another—and perhaps the crucial—form of dialogue and
adaptation is that which must be employed as the numbers of
local clergy increase. For many missionaries this may be the real
testing-ground of Christian idealism and generosity, as they
hand over, move on, move down the ladder—whatever is
necessary for the greater good of the local church. As more and
more dioceses in mission territories progress to this situation,

missionaries need to make a clear and calm re-appraisal of their changed position in these new churches. We have happily arrived at the stage of partnership with our fellow-priests of the local church. This is in itself a reason for rejoicing. In fact, it is not always easy to see why we are not more jubilant. Perhaps it is simply a human reaction to the fact that, in becoming partners, we almost automatically become junior partners. Our original position of command is over. But old attitudes die hard —and a sensitive local clergy do not always make things easy for us. But what do our missionary ideals mean if we fail to translate them into practical terms? The true partnership that both the local clergy and the missionaries work towards and desire can be brought into being only by our total surrender to the lordship of Christ; it is his glory that matters, not ours.

It is unwise to make too sharp a distinction between 'local clergy' and 'missionaries'. The oneness of the presbyterium of a diocese is a profound fact of the priestly life, and as missionaries we must, by exhortation and example, help to bring it fully into action. Our complete and unqualified partnership with the local clergy, for whose formation we worked, can be the beginning of a rich and fertile association in the missionary endeavour. As a result, we may be less militantly missionary, but we can be more persuasively missionary.

We go out to mission territories as ambassadors of a missionary Church which is also, following her Master's example, a servant Church. We offer our service, our diakonia, to the fledgeling churches we work in. Speaking of the missionary approach to non-Christian religions, Fr Amalorpavadass wrote:

> What diakonia do the religions require and which the Church can render? It is a diakonia of salvation, in keeping with the mission of the Church which is one of salvation ... It is a humble diakonia, a participation in the very diakonia of Christ to the Father and to the world. Hence we are not

supposed to put on an air of superiority and perform it as an act of condescension. Service is essentially humble and forgetful of self.

We must not consider the (non-Christian) religions as a virgin soil where we are the first ones to work, starting from scratch. We must not consider them as tabula rasa, and pretend to start from zero. We must be aware that we enter a place where others are present, where others have laboured, namely, God and men animated by Him.

Service must be relevant, and relevance is determined by the needs and requests, aspirations and desires of those whom we want to serve. Sometimes, religions as well as men may not be aware of their real needs; in such a case, it is incumbent on us to bring about this awareness, whether they be followers of religion or no religion. Christians 'should exert themselves lest modern man, overly intent on the science and technology of today's world, become a stranger to things divine. Rather, let them awaken in him a fiercer yearning for that truth and charity which God has revealed' (*Ad Gentes*, art. 11).

This missionary partnership in the service of the young churches must, however, be a partnership in the real sense of the word. It would be a lamentable lack of progress to replace one form of autocracy by another. Missionaries will be the first to rejoice when a particular church no longer needs them, but as long as it does and as long as they work there, their motives and their merits should be respected. We do not ask for privileges, but we do have rights. This is why the concept of partnership is now being expressed in practical terms by official detailed contracts—at the wish of the Congregation for the Evangelisation of Peoples. These contracts, signed between individual bishops and missionary institutes, are intended to ensure a more efficient deployment of the available resources of manpower and talent of the institutes, and to cater more efficiently for the needs and the possibilities of the individual dioceses. Contracts thus help the pastoral progress of mission dioceses and also help the institutes to marshal their resources more effectively and prepare their members for specific apostolic needs.

There are those who say, and even with a certain glee, that the day of the missionary institutes is over. It is hardly necessary to feel disturbed by the baleful prophecy, not even by the apparent glee. As Jean Guitton has said: 'Public opinion will always rejoice when sails are trimmed, when an appeal to heroism becomes uncertain, when something great fades away.'

The continuing need for missionary institutes has already been discussed, but a few further relevant remarks may be added. First, it is difficult to see how, in an age so dedicated to the concept of specialisation, a missionary, who is by definition a specialist in evangelisation, can be trained for his particular task if missionary institutes do not arrange to provide such training. It may be true to say that the institutes have not always prepared their members as well as they might have, but surely the lesson from this is obvious. A more scientific and specialised formation may involve a high degree of co-operation and pooling of resources in the 'home countries'. The seminary programme for future missionaries is currently the subject of deep and agonising examination, and clearly some radical changes and improvements will result.

Again, it is interesting to note that the value of such organisations as missionary institutes, especially in terms of continuity and efficiency, is being recognised more and more by other Christian Churches. In his book, *Missions in a Time of Testing*, Rev. Ronald K. Orchard advocates Protestant 'orders of missionaries'. Such an order 'would require of those who joined it a clear and definite calling to special service in the focal point of Mission, the proclamation of the Name where it has not been heard or is not acknowledged, and a willingness to be committed to that task without reservation, to receive whatever training the task required, and to go into any geographical area or area of human living to serve wherever there was a need in Mission which they could fulfil'.

A missionary should be an idealist, but should not be a starry-eyed one. He continually hopes for miracles, but is not shattered when they do not materialise. We must not expect that existing ecclesiastical structures can be replaced by smoothly-running and fully-functioning new ones in a day or a year—or even a decade. 'The Church essentially missionary' is a magnificent insight and a fine phrase, but only on condition that it is not allowed to remain a type of political slogan—full of bright promise but with no visible results. It is true that *Lumen Gentium* states clearly: 'The responsibility to proclaim the gospel throughout the world falls primarily on the body of bishops' (art. 29). But, as we have suggested already, can the college of bishops possibly be expected to take over the tasks of the missionary institutes? Obviously not in the foreseeable future; as we know, even a national episcopal conference can be a slow-moving and unwieldy piece of administrative machinery. A missionary bishop, having taken part in the Council debates on collegiality, had some blunt words to say in an article in *Vivante Afrique*: 'Many will think, in all good faith, that episcopal collegiality will solve everything, almost by magic. But we who live in the outposts know, and have known for many years, that the Christian world doles out missionary vocations in scanty rations. And now, in a great burst of enthusiasm, the bishops intend to share collegially in the evangelisation of the world . . . Two remarks come to mind. First, is it not when everybody has the task of closing a door that most often it is left open? Second, collegiality, which could give a great impetus to evangelisation, could equally deliver the *Coup-de-grâce*.'

We may not necessarily be quite as pessimistic as this, but it is well to remember that the great missionary advances of the past hundred years have been made possible chiefly by the new missionary institutes. A central agency can plan, can suggest, but who will go out to the mission territories to live and work and accept the daily drudgery? It is interesting to notice a rather similar fear being voiced by a high lay official of the Church of England: 'The truth is that some areas of life and action lend themselves to official centralisation, and some do not, and it is not always easy to distinguish. So men save themselves the trouble of thinking it all out and of accepting their own proper responsibility by pouring it all into the maw of the great machine—the central organisation with its vast administrative hopper. Official centralisation is popular today, partly because things are so very complicated, but partly because it suits an age of—shall I say, large and rather stuffy organisation. In such an age, it is easier to administer than to create, and the bureaucrat tends to supersede the pioneer. But a society conceived and brought forth for the preaching of the Gospel must have an inexhaustible capacity for breaking bounds; if it ceases to have this, it is ready to perish.'

All this quite clearly points to the need of the missionary institutes to continue devoting their recruiting, their training, their personnel, their missionary traditions and expertise, the impressive sum-total of their accumulated experience, to the service of a missionary Church that genuinely needs them.

What manner of man must the missionary of today be? We have seen, from many points of view, how much is demanded of him—and it is a lot. He is expected to be familiar with many areas of thought and activity that were no concern of his predecessors. But in our anxiety to equip the young missionary with new knowledge and skills, are we relegating, to an alarmingly inadequate secondary position, the key factor: the orientation of his whole personality to God? Not merely has the missionary's spiritual formation not kept pace with the wider range and improved methods of intellectual formation, but it seems to have been almost entirely excluded by increasingly heavier schedules and the current epidemic of confusion. However, no matter how archaic it may sound, a venerable principle of Christian education and action has not lost its truth: 'Scientia sine caritate inflat; caritas sine scientia errat; scientia cum caritate aedificat.'

The appeal of *Ad Gentes* could hardly be more eloquent: 'Imbued with a living faith and a hope that never fails, the missionary should be a man of prayer. He should glow with a spirit of strength and of love and of self-discipline . . . Let him in the spirit of sacrifice always bear about in himself the dying of Jesus, so that the life of Jesus may work in those to whom he is sent. Out of zeal for souls, let him gladly spend all and be spent himself for souls' (art. 25). Everyone accepts all this in principle, but to what extent have missionary institutes, in their formation programmes, attempted to turn it into practice?

A missionary spirituality capable of serenely confronting the multiple pressures of our day will certainly depend on one cardinal question: are a man's personal motive and his daily life Christ-centred? And from this point of view do we simply demand enough of ourselves?

Towards the end of 1969 Pro Mundi Vita organised a colloquium at Louvain on the theme 'Restructuring of Missionary Formation'. The report of the discussions makes extremely interesting reading. For example, on the subject of motivation:

> There are furthermore the variety of motivations, concepts and attitudes of the present candidates. The latter contest not so much the Church as its function in the world as sacrament of Salvation. They wish to work for development without labelling this activity as a work of the Catholic or Protestant Church.

They have a horror of any neo-colonialism, whether political, economic, cultural or religious. They wish to be present in a helping capacity. They no longer like to speak of the 'third world', they prefer international solidarity; they do not wish to go to 'aid', but 'to go to meet another man'. They reject furthermore the division West—Third World. They wish to be the men of communication, diffusers of information . . .

Their personal motives are very varied. There are sociological motives: desire for change, compassion, social interests, desire to escape, love of travelling, desire for self-realisation. Some wish to 'peregrinare pro Christo', or wish to respond to the social encyclicals and to *Populorum Progressio*, some are seeking a direct and explicit evangelisation, others a life of Christian witness, others yet again a co-operation in economic development (the relations between evangelisation and development are moreover not clear to them) . . . Many of their motivations must be inadequate, for they are not sufficient to retain a certain proportion in the receiving country.

This section of the report concludes with the warning: 'A very serious personal motivation is necessary to sustain the activity of the missionary. Good motives, such as compassion, social interest, must be broadened and deepened. The less good and the frankly inadequate motives, such as love of travel, taste for adventure, running away, must be replaced. Self-realisation is a questionable motive.'

Even the most perfect motive can survive only if nourished by a man's personal experience of God's love and his total response to it. In talking of spiritual formation, the report says: 'The life of prayer demands particular attention: the new liturgy has still not prepared replacements for the former structures of the life of prayer. The young people also feel a certain reticence towards the diverse traditional forms of asceticism; they seek it mainly in various forms of activity. Spirituality will have to respect the pluralism of missionary motivations. But the different "spiritualities" of the various missionary or religious institutes are regarded with great reserve by the young.'

Considerable reserve toward a multiplicity of 'spiritualities' (but does this exist?) is understandable, but what if it subtly becomes a reserve towards spirituality itself?

We must prepare ourselves for the hard facts of the missionary situation as it is. We are missionaries in the second half of the twentieth century, not in the simpler, more romantic and individualistic seventeenth century. We are coping with problems, but also with opportunities, beyond the wildest dreams of our predecessors. Missionary activity does not grow easier with the changing circumstances and rapid advances of the local churches; in some respects it grows more difficult and makes greater demands on the expatriate missionary. A missionary needs to be unselfish—and we can sink self only by enthroning Christ at the heart of our lives and our work. If our work, no matter what form it takes, is not directed explicitly and constantly to Christ, if it is not being done for his greater glory and the accomplishment of his lordship, for how long can we continue to do it? A missionary's love for God must be expressed *through* his work, not outside of it or in spite of it.

He needs to cultivate a grateful awareness of the privilege of being God's fellow-worker, 'God's helper in spreading the Good News of Christ' (1 *Thess.* 3:2). He needs a reverent and finely-honed appreciation of the wonderful message he carries —the unique and timeless and saving Good News. This is the witness to Christ which forms our missionary speciality. There is little use in being 'a man of communication' if we have nothing to communicate. Jean Guitton has written: 'Faith, in an age that is so demanding as regards proof, needs witnesses.

Now the witness is he who stakes his life.' 'Who stakes his life'—how thoroughly can this be verified, for example, in a cautiously calculated temporary acceptance of missionary status hedged around by multiple, and mainly selfish, qualifications and conditions?

Obviously, the missionary's witness to Christ will be by life as well as by word. When it comes to attracting men to Christ, if we are to follow in St Paul's footsteps and tell them 'about Jesus, and only about him as the crucified Christ' (1 Cor. 2:2), we must do so by more than words. The missionary is a professional purveyor of the word—but he is also a professional liver of the word, because he is a witness. No one more so than the pastoral missionary, and this honour no 'expert' or 'specialist' can take from him. In the current clamour for the application of scientific methods to missionary problems there is a tendency to underestimate the value, the dignity and the necessity of the pastoral missionary. One wonders if there is not a condescending and slightly disparaging tone in articles which refer to the average missionary as 'a pastoral factotum'.

The missionary of today needs to be a patient man, because 'the seeds of the Word' sprout slowly, and we must depend on the Lord of the harvest to give the increase; we are merely his labourers. The biblical account of the salvation story is enough to convince us that God is infinitely patient; we must attempt to imitate him. The journey from Old Testament image to New Testament reality was a slow one, with many hesitations and quite a few reverses. The salvation story has not really changed its tempo since. Men and nations move towards Christ, but only slowly—and we cannot hasten the growth of faith in the heart of a man. We must not be too easily discouraged by apparent lack of results; we must not be avaricious for comforting statistics. As Canon Taylor has written: 'What matters to a missionary at the end of the day is neither the task nor the outcome but the One with whom and for whom he goes forward.'

The missionary of today needs to be a humble man, because his work is hard and often hidden, and he must not depend on plaudits from his flock—or his superiors. The schoolboy image of a missionary surrounded by an admiring and unalterably grateful flock is apt to suffer a rude shock when college students go on strike for later hours out the town, or parishioners refuse to come to a new church because they feel it should have been built elsewhere. It is in circumstances such as these that motives are tested. Only one motive will sustain us: that our missionary work is an act of love of God and an act of obedience to Christ's command. Much of the missionary's daily grind involves work that is hidden and mostly unappreciated; he often works in little bush parishes where there is no companion to encourage him, where there is no deadline to meet. Only a deep personal ambition to share the treasures of redemption with everyone he finds will urge him to continue the quiet unobtrusive task of ministering Christ's charity. And like Christ, he must do it unostentatiously. Christ did not become, or seek to become, an international figure—but day after day he radiated his charity to whatever little circle of farmers, fishermen, children or sinners he found about him.

Changing times and circumstances will call on us to make many alterations in our missionary methods and approaches. But the man is more important than the methods—and only a man of Christ, in the full sense of that phrase, can make an effective missionary. Not only a man of Christ, but a man constantly aware that it is Christ who calls men and enlightens them, and that we are only his fumbling instruments. And though we are obliged in conscience to be as scientific and as efficient as possible, in the last analysis it is our personal goodness and kindness and sincerity that will lead people to reach out for the healing grace of Christ.

Because Christ is the Lord of the universe, and we go forth mantled by his promise to be with us always, the missionary is an eternal optimist. His hope is based, not on his own efforts or their results, but on what Christ can do through him. And this is a hope that never deceives. We may often be frustrated by the thoughtlessness and malice of men, but hope will help us to contemplate with equanimity the perennial paradox of divine love and human liberty. The founders of missionary institutes saw darker days than ours, but they did not surrender to discouragement. Our predecessors on the missions lived through greater hardships, and their graves lie dotted along every missionary coastline of the world, so that we might reap where they sowed. If we are fearful, is it not for the same reason as the shaken men in the boat on Lake Tiberias—because we are 'men of little faith'?

APPENDIX a)

MISSION THEOLOGY FOR OUR TIMES
A Symposium sponsored by SEDOS

Official text of conclusions

THE WHY OF MISSION

Missionaries have always been convinced of the urgent necessity of mission towards non-Christians. But in our days this conviction is being put to the test.

In many countries where on the one hand the population keeps constantly growing, conversions diminish and even, in certain instances, become or remain impossible. At the same time, an evolution of thought is taking place which tends to acknowledge the positive role which non-Christian religions can play in the journey which leads towards the salvation acquired once and for ever in Jesus Christ. Thus a great number of questions are posed: must we now still work at all costs for the conversion of non-Christians and for their entrance into the Church? Would it not be better simply to help non-Christians to grow and go forward in their own religions? Will not conversion to the Christian faith merely uproot them? In any event, what can serve today as the true 'incentive' for missionary activity?

a. Non-Christian Religions and Salvation in Jesus Christ

It will be helpful, on this point, to recall certain truths.

1. The holy Spirit is at work in the heart of every man and in the midst of people. But to the extent that the non-Christian religions are creations of the religious genius of man as he seeks his own destiny, these religions cannot be ways of salvation since the unique way of salvation proceeds from the initiative of the Father: this is Christ, known by faith, and accepted in love.

2. Nonetheless the non-Christian religions do contain authentic values and thus constitute a true preparation for the gospel, even if these religions contain also an admixture of errors and deviations. Purified and elevated by grace, these authentic values may constitute a means for those following non-Christian religions of coming to the act of faith and of charity which is necessary for salvation. But we must not rule out the possibility that in these religions there may be found, in their beliefs and in their rites, supernatural elements—from whatever source they may derive.

3. The existence of non-Christian religions, far from rendering useless the proclamation of the gospel, really provides a new argument for its abiding importance. To state that these non-Christian religions may serve as preparations for the gospel, is to state that there exists in them an ordering unto Christ—a thrust towards Christ— which only the proclamation of the gospel can bring to fulfilment. If supernatural elements are to be found in these religions, they should be led back to their source, and led forward to their fullness, which is the Word incarnate living within the Church.

b.   Why the Missions then?

In the perspective we have here adopted, the missions remain fully justified.

1. If the grace of God given to men for their salvation ordains them to Christ, it is the *mission* which allows men (within the conditions wherein they find themselves) to go forward till they arrive at the full knowledge of the mystery of Christ.

2. It is the *mission* which reveals to men their true nature, their destiny and the ultimate meaning of their lives, the means of effectively bringing about the realisation of their longings for unity and peace (aspirations which are in fact the fundamental concerns of mankind today).

3. If Christ has given the Church this mandate of proclaiming throughout the world the glad tidings of his resurrection and of everywhere bringing into play the newness of the gospel, it is so that all things may be progressively placed under the sway of Christ's rule and Lordship. When missionaries invite all peoples to make their choice of Christ and to become his disciples, they labour for the glory of God, the Church reveals the true meaning of her catholicity, and the way is prepared for the eschatological fulfilment of the kingdom of God.

c.   Missionary approaches

In the area of attitudes and concrete ways of acting, certain points are worth making here.

1. The missionaries never begin from zero. It is of importance that, through dialogue, they discover the authentic values which are present in non-Christian religions so that these values may be purified and elevated and the gospel of Christ introduced into them. Thus Christ will be made manifest to non-Christians, that he may appear to them, not as a stranger, but as the one whom they have always sought for: 'quod ignorantes quaeritis, hoc ego annuntio vobis' (He whom without knowing you have been seeking, He it is whom I now proclaim to you) (*Acts* 17:23).

2. So that a genuine dialogue may be set up and may prove truly fruitful, the fulfilment of several conditions is absolutely necessary:

a) the missionaries, both priests and laypeople, should really and truly enter into the cultures of the non-Christian peoples so that they may understand them *from within* and that—with regard to those to whom they are sent—they may encounter them as they are, within the very heart, even, of their own religious experience (and sensibility);

b) missionary dispensation—the reality of the existence and history of the missionary—must somehow reproduce within itself the mystery of Christ himself, which mystery is a dispensation of incarnation, death and resurrection;

c) the conversion of individual persons must be seen within the larger perspectives of the conversion of entire peoples and the perspective of the salvation of all mankind.

MISSION AND DEVELOPMENT

Genuine missionaries have always worked for the growth and development of mankind. So long as this effort was expended within the limits of a parish or a diocese, no special problem presented itself. But today the organisation of development has become a much more complex affair; it has assumed the dimensions of whole nations, of entire continents, of the wide world itself. It has become a task for specialists, and the ordinary missionaries run the danger of no longer seeing and understanding the role they are called on to play in the task of development.

The theology of mission and development should help them to bring into practice a fidelity to their missionary vocation of evangelisation and of the fostering of the full growth of man within this new framework of development. But often enough they have the impression that the mission of Christ has been drowned, submerged in a great technical or human enterprise, instead of being its soul and its force.

They stand in perplexity when faced with the contradictory opinions of theologians. If some theologians insist on the primordial and irreplaceable character of the proclamation of God's word and of the sacramental ministry, missionaries who are—by the demands of the situations in which they find themselves and the concrete needs they encounter—taken up with the tasks of development, are troubled by an uneasy conscience. If other theologians stress the primary role of development, then those missionaries whose tasks are those which belong to the more traditional patterns of the apostolate, begin to question the value of what they are doing.

The principal difficulties which face missionaries may be grouped around those questions which the theologians of the symposium have tried to give answers to.

a. The Relationship between Evangelisation and Development

By the word development we mean what the encyclical *Populorum Progressio* means: we are dealing with integral development, that is, the development of the whole of man and the development of all men. This is first of all the working out of the new commandment of the gospel: 'As Christ has loved you, love one another.' In this perspective, work undertaken to further integral development is a genuine means of evangelisation. Its thrust goes beyond the temporal; this work, taken concretely, is a task which involves the whole of man, a task which demands a radical option of his spiritual freedom.

To the extent that this task involves man, development becomes a reality which is not merely an 'object lesson'; it is a living and eloquent witness of the Lordship of Christ over the world. This witnessing should be acknowledged as a work of evangelisation in its strict sense, as an act which is explicitly religious. This witness, which is one of the ways of carrying out evangelisation, requires in turn the proclamation of the genuine word of salvation, thus revealing to men the mystery of our divine calling and answering 'the problems and longings of the man of today'.

A necessary bond thus exists between the two ways of evangelisation. The second way, the ministry of the word and the sacraments, reveals to men the deepest, the ultimate meaning of development, and gives to it a dynamism which is no longer a merely human thing. To the extent that Christians are the visible instruments of the mediation of Christ, they render an irreplaceable service to the task of development. For one's acceptance of, and faithfulness to the word give one a new sense—a new understanding—of one's responsibility for the history and adventure of man, which are seen as a unity.

Wherever the personal preaching of the word is not possible, the task of development, inspired by this spirit, retains a truly missionary significance. It contributes to the realisation of the kingdom of God in all its dimensions, but—from the very first —the missionary must intend this, and must above all see that his witness is an eloquent one in all he does and is. For Christ 'began to do and to teach'.

b. The Role of the Church as Institute of Salvation

The whole contribution of the Church to the task of development should be rendered in a spirit of service and not of paternalism. 'I have come, not to be served, but to serve.'

It is in the light of this principle that one must decide as to the opportunities of setting up or keeping alive certain institutions and as to the desirability of involvement in ways and structures which are not those of the Church itself.

In any case, in this area, the role of the Church is a role of education, whose purpose is that communities may at length be vivified by that love which has its ultimate source in Christ.

c. Should we Project to other Continents the Secularisation of the West?

From Africa and Asia we gather the impression on the one hand that the phenomenon of secularisation has begun to manifest itself in all its ambiguity, and on the other hand that non-Christians put forth increasing efforts to integrate earthly tasks within their religious perspectives.

We can nonetheless hope that the genius proper to these continents will preserve them from certain extremes which the West has already experienced.

In this context, it is important that we keep before our minds the distinction, in practice so easily forgotten, between secularisation and secularism.

Secularisation, rightly understood, acknowledges the 'proper autonomy' of earthly realities (*Gaudium et Spes*, art. 36) without endangering the ultimate orientation and thrust of all human activity.

APPENDIX b)

List of theologians

D. A. AMALORPAVADASS

Bangalore, India. Doctor of theology at the Institut Catholique, Paris. Director of the All-India Catechetical Centre at Bangalore.

Among his publications: *Destinée de l'Église dans l'Inde d'aujourd'hui* (Paris 1967).

ARNULPHUS CAMPS

Franciscan, born in 1925 at Eindhoven (Holland). Studied at Nijmegen and Fribourg Universities. Doctorate in 1957. Professor of missiology in Karachi (Pakistan) and Nijmegen (Holland).

JEAN DANIÉLOU

Jesuit, doctor of theology. Professor at the Theological Faculty of Paris; dean of this Theological Faculty since 1962.

Among his publications:
> *Platonisme et théologie mystique* (1944),
> *Essai sur le mystère de l'histoire* (1953),
> *God and Us* (1961),
> *Scandaleuse vérité* (1961),
> *Prayer as a Political Problem* (1968).

HERMAN A. M. FIOLET

Born in Amsterdam 1920. Has a doctorate in theology from the University of Nijmegen and is at present a professor of dogmatic theology. Has published several books including one on ecumenism.

JEAN FRISQUE

Born in 1925 in Belgium. Member of Society of Mission Auxiliaries. Professor of ecclesiology at the Mission de France Major Seminary (Limoges). Has written extensively on the thought of Oscar Cullman.

JOSE-MARIA GONZALEZ-RUIZ

Born in Spain in 1916 and ordained in 1939. He studied in Rome at the Gregorian University and at the Biblical Institute. Doctor of theology in 1940 and licentiate in Sacred Scripture in 1953. Professor of New Testament studies at the Pontifical University of Salamanca (Spain).

Among his publications:
El Evangelio de Pablo (Madrid 1963),
El Cristianismo no es un humanismo (Barcelona 1966),
Pobreza evangelica y promocion humana (Barcelona 1966).

DOMENICO GRASSO

Jesuit, born in Italy; was ordained in 1947. Since 1950 professor of pastoral theology at the Pontifical Gregorian University, Rome. Consultor of the Sacred Congregation of the Council.

Among his publications:
Gesu Cristo e la sua opera (1957),
Il primato di Pietro (1962),
Ci sarà una sola Chiesa (1962),
L'annunzio della salvezza (1965).

STANISLAUS LYONNET

Jesuit, born in 1902 at Saint-Etienne (France); ordained in 1934, professor at the Pontifical Biblical Institute, Rome. Dean of the Biblical Faculty.

Among his publications:
Les Épitres de saint Paul aux Galates, aux Romains (3rd ed. 1969),
Theologia biblica Novi Testamenti; de Peccato et Redemptione (2nd ed. 1960),
La storia della salvezza nella lettera ai Romani (1966).

JOHN SCHUTTE

Born in Essen 1913. Ordained as member of the Society of the Divine Word in 1936. Missionary in China until his expulsion in 1952 after seven months of solitary confinement. Doctorate in theology of missiology. Superior General of SVD 1958-1967. Several books and articles on missiological questions.

OTTO SEMMELROTH

Jesuit, born in Germany in 1912; ordained in 1939. Doctor of theology (Bonn University) in 1947. Since 1949 professor of dogma at the Theological Faculty, Frankfurt.

Among his publications:
Die Kirche als Ursakrament (3rd ed. 1963),
Das geistliche Amt (2nd ed. 1965).

THARCISSE TSHIBANGU

Born in the Congo in 1933. Rector of the Lovanium University at Kinshasa. Doctorate in theology from Louvain. Many articles on African theology and religious thought.